AUSTRAL SPANISH KNIGHT

V.J.A. Flynn,
Jyshwick,
Aust". Cap". Territory,
13 - 1. '13

AUSTRALIA'S SPANISH KNIGHT

FOURTEEN MONTHS
SIXTY ONE YEARS

D.L. SPEIGHT

AUSTRALIA'S SPANISH KNIGHT

Copyright © D.L. and K.L. Speight 2004

Published by D.L. and K.L. Speight
6 Pine Avenue, Seacliff, S.A. 5049 Australia
Tel. (08) 8298 1945

National Library of Australia
Cataloguing-in-Publication entry:

Speight, D. Lawrence (Desmond Lawrence), 1935- .
Australia's Spanish Knight : fourteen months, sixty-one years.

Bibliography.
ISBN 0 646 44123 X

I. Bryant, Richard, 1911-2003. I. Title.

920

Erratum
Page 129, Line 17 should read:
"*eastwards* towards Belchite..."

Printed by Hyde Park Press, Adelaide, South Australia

To Joan

They went because
their open eyes
could see no other way

ACKNOWLEDGEMENTS

- Richard Bryant for allowing me to record his life's experiences and for answering my endless questions about details of incidents and events.
- Arturo Reig Tapia, former Spanish Consul General to Australia, for his encouragement and assistance in Spain.
- John and Judy Dally for reading the original manuscript and making suggestions with respect to language and presentation.
- Alun Kenwood for comments on the historical background covered in 'Fourteen Months' and for his encouragement to keep going with the project.
- John Mallon for comments on characterisation and the description of historical events in 'Fourteen Months'.
- Maureen and Dermot Moriarty for their comments on the manuscript.
- Members of the Casino at Colmenar de Oreja, staff of the Ayuntamiento de Brunete, Marcelino Valdes of the Huete Tourist Office, Agustín García of the Teruel Tourist Office and his friend Carlos Abril for their information and generous assistance.
- Duncan and Gloria Bryant for information with respect to the Australia section of 'Sixty One Years' and for the photographs of Joan and the Brigader badge.
- The staff of the State Library of South Australia and the Battye Library of West Australian History for their assistance in searching for obscure information.
- My wife Kate for interpreter services in Spain and also along with daughter Tasha for typing and correcting the manuscript and making suggestions with respect to English expression.
- My son-in-law Sam, son Conrad, and friends Jenny Clift and Jenny Peterson for providing computer assistance.
- Paula Schetters for redrawing maps.
- Marx Memorial Library, London, for ambulance photograph used on back cover.

PREFACE

Australia's Spanish Knight is drawn from the recorded recollections of Richard Bryant who was born in South Shields, England, in 1911. His recollections are unlikely to have been exaggerated or embellished with the passage of time as he has told the same stories to family and friends throughout his long life.

In writing this book about the life of Richard Bryant, I have made every effort to present as correct a historical context as possible to the events and incidents in which he was involved. I have in places in the narrative used conversations to highlight his recollections and experiences, and to bring those with whom he had dealings more into the picture.

For the record, Richard Bryant's original surname was Smith, which he changed to Bryant in 1961, before taking up Australian citizenship.

Des Speight

CONTENTS

FOURTEEN MONTHS

		Page
1.	Brunete, Spain - July 1937	3
2.	Huete	6
3.	The road to Madrid	19
4.	Leaving Huete	51
5.	Teruel	61
6.	The Blizzard	72
7.	Teruel again	105
8.	Aragón	128
9.	Catalonia	151
10.	Back to Blighty	156
11.	Barcelona	162
12.	London	174

SIXTY ONE YEARS

13.	England - 1938	179
14.	Palestine and Iraq - 1946	187
15.	Qatar - 1948	196
16.	Sudan - 1951	201
17.	Adelaide, Australia - 1956	208
18.	Gibson Desert and Anna Plains	215
19.	Maralinga	227
20.	Elizabeth	231
21.	Brighton	235
22.	Spain remembers	238

ILLUSTRATIONS

- Map I   Spanish Locations   1937 - 1938   246
- Map II   Ports of Call   1926 - 1935   247
- Map III   Palestine and Iraq Locations 1946 - 1948   248
- Map IV   Qatar and Sudan Locations   1948 - 1955   249
- Map V   Australian Locations   1956 - 2000   250

BIBLIOGRAPHY   251

FOURTEEN MONTHS

I

BRUNETE, SPAIN
July 1937

The road to the front was no more than a narrow dirt track. The ruts made in it by mule carts during the winter rains were now concrete troughs and ridges long hardened by the relentless summer sun. Heat shimmered off its surface making vision uncertain as did the dust kicked up by moving transport. Littered irregularly on either side was a miscellany of abandoned, wrecked and sometimes charred vehicles bearing witness to the dangers of using the road. Beyond the wrecks glared the parched expanses of the Meseta, relieved only by a scattering of dark dwarf oaks shaped like giant mushrooms on bent spindly stalks. And in the distance the cool green pine forests of the Sierra de Guadarrama beckoned through the haze.

Richard had long lost count of how many times he had bumped the ambulance along this road between the front lines and the transfer post in the rear. Now he was returning empty to the first aid post near Mosquito Hill. He was supporting a major Republican offensive to cut off the supply routes to the Fascist forces laying seige to Madrid. He cast a cursory glance at the abandoned pill-boxes which straddled the road and wondered how long they had held up the Republican advance. Not long, he thought. Just ahead the still smouldering ruins of Brunete seemed to confirm that. He hoped the women and children had managed to escape before the shelling and bombing began. As he worked the gears and the wheel to keep the vehicle on the road his mind turned to reports that although much territory had been taken in the early phase of the campaign, the Fascists had rallied. He had just heard that Dr. Sollenberger had been killed in the front-lines. He pictured his jovial bearded face, a face he would never see again. Now his thoughts turned to others he knew well in the Fifteenth Brigade out there in front of him; all volunteers, like himself, in the struggle to defeat fascism. They were facing ever-increasing enemy fire power, the sound of which was growing louder and louder as he drove towards it. This was all too familiar to him and he had learned to cope with the fear. He was committed. He had a job to do and the means to do it. He had to get through. There would be comrades to evacuate. Some would be Americans. They were taking a pounding.

There was a sudden flurry of activity well ahead of him. Through the swimming haze and dust vehicles were abruptly leaving the road and figures were dashing for the ditches which paralleled it. As this activity was some distance away, Richard didn't feel in immediate danger. He pulled the ambulance on to the side and jumped out to see if he could spot the enemy aircraft which he was sure was the cause of the commotion. Shading his eyes to get a better view he still had not sighted the aircraft when, engulfed in a hot surging wave, he was thrown into the air.

He could not have been unconscious for long because when he came round there was still no one near him. When he tried to get up he collapsed. Blood was streaming from his mouth, nose and ears. On his hands and knees he started crawling towards the ditch.

Something in his fogged brain told him that was the direction of safety. But he didn't even make that short distance. He collapsed again.

Richard never found out who rescued the rescuer. When he came to he was on a stretcher in an ambulance. There was a nurse tending him. She was washing the blood and sweat from his face. He drifted in and out of consciousness. When he was awake he hurt everywhere, inside and out. Nevertheless, he drew comfort from just the fact that he was alive and was being looked after and also that his rucksack and rifle had been put in the ambulance with him. His automatic and Brigade service book were in the rucksack.

"There, did I see you smile ?" asked the nurse.

2

HUETE

The hospital at Huete was mostly staffed by British volunteers. It was on the eastern edge of the small compact town and housed in a recently abandoned monastery. A good choice as even the Fascists would think twice about bombing the historic Monasterio de Santa María, not that it wouldn't have been an easy target. It was a prominent three storey sandstone building and from the valley was almost fortress-like in appearance. Its dormitories, washrooms, kitchens, dining rooms and halls suited it well as a hospital. Also its inner courtyards afforded places where convalescing soldiers could exercise and medical staff find temporary escape from dealing with the wounded and the dying. For a few, solace might be found in its large stone chapel which faced into the town and opened onto the Plaza de la Merced.

The British volunteers included Nan Green, the hospital administrator, Tudor Hart, the chief surgeon, the nurses and Nathan Clark, the transport manager. They were all English while Thomas Kerr, the *tendencia*, quartermaster, who looked after supplies was Irish. Local Spanish people from the town were also involved in the hospital, assisting with the catering and upkeep of the place and providing the major part of the food needs of the patients and staff.

For a week after his arrival at Huete, Richard was kept in an upstairs intensive care ward which catered for up to twenty serious cases. Tudor Hart's examination of him had revealed no broken bones, no ruptured organs and miraculously, no shrapnel. But being thrown into the air by an exploding bomb and then dropping to the ground like a brick had jarred every bone, joint, organ and tissue in his body. He was watched around the clock for the first part of the week. As the days went by the bruising began to subside and he was able to sit up and feed himself, and soon he wanted to get up and walk around. He was transferred to the ground floor convalescent ward where he could enjoy the company of others and enjoy strolling in the courtyard in the morning and evenings. The midday sun was escaped indoors. Siesta time. The other convalescents were mostly nursing more visible injuries. Some were amputees. His rapid recovery had undoubtedly been assisted by his fitness. His enthusiasm for exercising had started in the gymnastic team at the Gateshead school he was sent to, an enthusiasm that had kept him fit during his years of service in the merchant navy. When he presented himself for service in Spain he was a strong, wiry, confident twenty five year old. Below a shock of brown hair, his grey eyes gazed steadily from a handsome face which already showed lines of experience. He knew what he was about, and for that matter, what the war was about.

As Richard's mobility improved he had the freedom to move about the hospital and in and around a town as yet undamaged by war. Walking briskly up and down the steep and twisting *calles*, streets, of Huete he soon regained his customary fitness and agility. The size of the town ensured that there were always new paths to explore and even the ones he knew well often seemed different with the ever changing play of sunlight and shadow. He became a familiar sight to the local people. Recognised by his badged beret as an International Brigades volunteer, there would always be someone to hail him with a 'Hola' from a wrought iron balconied window. He would look up and return the greeting with a grin and the clenched fist salute.

The climb out of the town through the low heath to the top of the hill which overlooked it had special rewards. From there he would gaze at the steep ranges of the Alcarria and the Serranía de Cuenca stretching to the horizon. Only to the South were plains to be seen, the plains of La Mancha. He would marvel at the endlessness of it all and closer to, at the red, brown, yellow and white layered ochres exposed in the hill-face across the valley. Sometimes the sight and sound of aircraft would break into his reverie. His thoughts would turn back to the war, to the threat of fascism and to why he was in Spain.

*   *   *

Much as Richard enjoyed his return to health, he couldn't cope with being idle. What he could do, he realised, was to help with the hospital's transport which was a mixture of four ambulances, four small vans and two supply lorries. And help was needed. The vehicles looked ramshackle, dented and dirty and only had anything done to them when they broke down. Moreover, they were parked in the plaza and *calles* outside the hospital where they could be damaged, have parts stolen, or simply be driven off. Theft of vehicles was a serious problem. They were sometimes commandeered by the militias who believed they had privileged property rights, or stolen for a quick getaway by deserters.

"What, you trained with Rolls Royce!" exclaimed Nathan Clark when Richard started to explain something about his experience with motor vehicles.

"Well that was after I'd done a special six month motor mechanics course at Wallsend. The Rolls Royce course was for chauffeurs, but it did include routine maintenance; you know, greasing, oil changing, adjusting brakes, even wheel balancing".

"So, did you become a chauffeur?"

"Not half!," he grinned. "To a London barrister. I used to drive him to the Old Bailey, and his wife to Harrods. I'd follow her round the store while she piled me up with parcels. I'd open the car door for her to get in and out, all togged up in my livery. I used to feel like a servant!"

Nathan roared laughing, picturing Richard, whose only concession to uniform now was his badged beret. "You all spruced up in a chauffeur's outfit, I can't believe it. I just can't believe it!"

"But they were really nice people," he cut in, thinking that he had conveyed an overly servile image of himself. "They treated me well. I used to take the car home at night, and sometimes would be allowed to have it for the weekend. I would service it and take my mother for a spin in the country."

"It just goes to show that some well-off people are decent."

"Well, you're right". His mind switched to the Earnshaws who ran the chemical manufacturing business at Welwyn Garden City where he was working before setting off for Spain. Mrs Earnshaw, the boss's wife, used to bring the workers mugs of cocoa or tea for morning or afternoon breaks. He'd never forget that. "You're well off yourself and you're here risking your life and living like a peasant", added Richard.

Nathan's middle class background showed through in both his demeanour and his speech and Richard knew that Nathan was one of the Clark shoe family. They were all Quakers, didn't believe in war, yet here was Nathan supporting one side of a war, although admittedly in a non-combatant role. But he never asked Nathan to explain that conundrum. He sensed it was too personal.

"I'm no hero," said Nathan bluntly, embarrassed by the thought that he had appeared to pay himself a compliment. "Anyway, there are quite a few well-off socialists in Britain."

*   *   *

After three weeks there, Richard was discharged from the convalescent ward and simply bunked down in an unused end of a long corridor. No one minded, particularly as he had started making himself useful working on the transport. But conditions for maintaining the vehicles remained poor. They were still all parked in the *calles* and in the plaza.

"What we need is a garage with an inspection pit." His comment as he wormed out from under one of the ambulances after doing an oil change was directed to Nathan.

"That would be ideal," responded Nathan sympathetically, "but we can't just conjure one up out of thin air."

"To hell with thin air. There's a place staring us in the face."

"What do you mean? What place?"

"The chapel!" Taking advantage of Nathan's speechlessness, he continued. "We can get local help to carry out the pews for free firewood or whatever, lift up a couple of the slate flags in the floor to make a pit. We could park all the vehicles in there at night and security would cease to be a problem."

"And how are you going to get them in there? You can't just drive into the chapel from the plaza even though the main doorway is big enough. There's a vestibule in the way."

"Oh! you mean that small entrance hall. I've thought of that. We could just knock a hole in the wall directly facing the doorway. Then our vehicles could be driven straight in. Local tradesmen could do the job." Nathan agreed it was a good plan and said he would seek approval to go ahead with it

Nan Green quickly agreed to the proposal. Nan was an attractive dynamic Londoner, with a natural air of authority which well suited her administrative role. The idea of housing the transport appealed to her straight away

"It's your idea Richard, so you're in charge," said Nathan, " You know what you want. The *tendencia* will find the tradesmen for you and they can dig the pit as well."

The work went ahead promptly, but one unforeseen complication occurred during the digging of the pit. About a metre and a half down, a skeleton was uncovered.

"Don't tell me there are nuns under all these flags," exclaimed Richard to one of the Spanish workmen who could speak some English.

"Yes, many, but only this one is a problem," was the response.

"What can we do?"

"I'll get the gravedigger to collect the skeleton and bury her in the cemetery. You will have to pay him."

When all the work was finished, the hospital staff came to inspect what had been done. Nathan said in jest that it was perhaps the most architecturally stunning garage in Spain. Its high vaulted ceiling and stained glass windows gave it a special aura. Thomas said that he wouldn't be surprised to come into the place one day soon and find Richard saying the rosary. They all laughed at the thought.

Nathan left soon after the garage was set up to return to Britain where he planned to address meetings to encourage support for the Republican cause. He wanted Richard to go with him, as he believed his experiences on the battlefronts would be of great assistance to his purpose, but he refused. When Nathan left, Tudor Hart appointed Richard transport manager. He ran a tight ship. When vehicles in use were returned to the garage, drivers handed in the keys and the garage was locked up at night. A young Irishman, recovering from his wounds, had volunteered to help him and although he knew little about vehicles, he was another pair of hands. Spare parts were a problem, but Richard could usually find what he wanted at the International Brigades workshop at Tarancón. Other times he would go to Cuenca for supplies. Both towns were within easy reach. Occasionally, he went as far as Valencia to obtain medical supplies. He always revelled in the freedom of driving across the open Meseta. It reminded him of the Pennine moorlands of Durham and Northumberland, but it wasn't the same.

*   *   *

The main relaxation for staff at the hospital was talk. Talk about what needed to be done. Talk about the progress of the war. Talk about where you came from. Talk about the depression and politics. Talk about personal involvement in the cause. There were two main talk shops. One was the staff dining and common room. There the talk was mainly about practicalities. The other was the garage, where two or three of the shorter pews had been left behind as if for that particular purpose. Here the talk was often more personal and wide-ranging. After evening meals, some of the staff would gravitate to the garage, perhaps to escape the atmosphere of the hospital, but more so to enjoy the talk. And there were principal talkers. Richard with his front-line ambulance experience had a fund of stories. Thomas the *tendencia*, a thin and sickly but outgoing Irishman, knew the local Spanish community well, could speak passable Spanish and consequently was a valuable source of unofficial news. And then there was Joan Harrison, a theatre nurse, recently posted from the Aragón front. She was a handsome woman with dark engaging eyes and olive complexion. And with her fine posture and dark hair she could have passed for one of the local women of Huete.

"Well, to tell you the truth," said Thomas, responding to a question as to how he had become a volunteer, "I was out of a job. And when I read that Fascists were trying to overthrow a popularly elected government, I thought I should do something useful with myself. It reminded me of the long struggle in Ireland to establish a republic. The English caught the leaders, rebels they called them, and either executed them or deported them to Australia."

"It wasn't really the English," interjected Joan indignantly, "it was the British government, the ruling class, who treated the Irish badly. They even let them starve in the potato famine." They all looked at Joan in surprise, as with her posh southern English boarding school accent she sounded as if she was of the ruling class herself. Undeterred, she added as if to bring the issue to a close, "And it is the British government now which is helping to defeat the Republic here through its so-called non-intervention policy."

"Well I won't argue with that," said Thomas.

And the others fell silent, fitting what Thomas and Joan had said into the jigsaws of their own experience and understanding.

"You wouldn't have been unemployed, Joan," echoed around the former chapel. It was Richard who had broken the silence with his Geordie twang. "There's always work for nurses. What brought you to Spain?"

"Florence Nightingale," said Joan abruptly and with a smile as if that answered the question. Everyone, in Britain at least, knew that Florence Nightingale had become a household name for looking after wounded soldiers. But it was all a long time ago. Faced with puzzled and expectant expressions, Joan went on. "Florence Nightingale became famous looking after wounded British soldiers in the Crimean War. That was in the middle of the last century. She was appalled by the almost complete lack of medical aid for the wounded. It was as if the army thought they were expendable once they could no longer fight. But she fought. She fought the top army brass to provide blankets and medical supplies and set up a well run hospital nursing the wounded back to health. Soon she was in charge of organising the nursing in a string of military hospitals in the Crimea. Countless lives were saved because of her efforts." She paused, but nobody said anything. Now she changed to a more explanatory tone of voice. "When we were in training at Barts hospital in London, we constantly had Florence Nightingale held up to us. We should all try to be like her, we were told. So here I am!"

"To be sure, you are like her," said Thomas.

But Richard had a faraway look . At last he spoke. "What you said Joan made me think of two Florence Nightingales I knew on the

Jarama front, working day and night in a makeshift hospital at Colmenar de Oreja. They were Australian nurses."

Again a silence. Soon he realised that they were all continuing to look in his direction. They were waiting for his tale on how he had become involved in the cause. He grinned. They all liked the way his handsome face under his brown tousled hair would break into a grin at the drop of a hat. He grinned because he thought he had a good tale to tell. But they had to wait until he worked out where to start.

"Last year I was driving lorries for a chemical firm in Welwyn Garden City. I used to take their drums of cellulose all over the place, to Nottingham, Huddersfield, Batley. And I used to service the vehicles back at the factory between trips. The boss was left-leaning even though he was a capitalist, and when the Fascist rebellion started here we discussed it a lot during the breaks. We all thought that Franco had to be stopped, but the government wasn't for doing anything, as you well know. When people started volunteering for the Republican cause, we talked about that as well."

"You did one hell of a lot of talking," interrupted Thomas.

"Most of the lads were married and had good jobs there and a decent boss. They would have been sacrificing a lot by going to Spain. I was different. For a start I was single, I didn't have any ties and." He paused collecting his thoughts. Now his voice was more reflective. The difference surprised them. "I suppose having been to many parts of the world during my time in the merchant navy; Russia, China, America, even Australia. Spain was not far away for me."

"I'll bet you don't think that now!," chimed in Thomas.

"Let him go on," said Joan, "we've heard about you."

Thomas cast a mock apologetic look at Richard.

"The place to go to volunteer was Communist Party headquarters in King Street in London."

Thomas thought, you didn't need to tell us that, but contained himself.

"It was December before I took the plunge. I was in London with the lorry and parked right outside the place. They took my name and address and asked a few other questions, then told me they would be in touch. One of the fellows came to the door to see me out. When I reached for my key to start up the lorry, he said with look of surprise on his face, 'Have you come in that?' 'Of course,' I replied. 'Well' he said, 'they're looking for ambulance drivers at Spanish Medical Aid. You could be driving yourself to Spain.' He told me where their office was. It wasn't too far away so I drove straight there. Spanish Medical Aid were keen, took my details and in January I got a letter telling me I was to join a convoy of four ambulances being sent to International Brigades headquarters at Albacete. I'd never heard of the place." And with an air of finality as if his tale was told, he added, "Anyway, we set off in February."

But Joan wanted to know what happened next; what the ambulances were like and if the journey was trouble free. He was flattered that she wanted to hear more. So he went on.

"As I said, there were four ambulances. They were big Bedfords, crammed full of medical supplies, blankets and comforts, mostly cigarettes and chocolates. You know, they had all been paid for by public subscription, and each had painted on the side where the subscriptions had come from. One was the Wales, another the

Holborn, I can't remember the other two. Anyway, we left London at the beginning of February. Each ambulance had two volunteers in the front and two or three in the back. I didn't know any of them. I presumed we were a mixture of drivers and medics. I was in the back of the Holborn with a fellow named Ted Fletcher. He was a Cambridge University student. Very refined he was, but strongly built," he added, as if it was unusual to be both.

"I thought you were supposed to be the driver?" questioned Thomas.

"I damn well wish that I had been! The fellow who was driving the Holborn was a real learner on the crash gear box. He hardly ever got it right. He jolted us all the way to the Channel coast and then all the way across France to Spain."

"You should have called him Jolt," said Thomas, and they all had a good laugh at that.

"So you didn't drive at all then?" queried Joan.

"I did. Just after the Figueres military base, I took over the Holborn and drove all the way to Albacete."

"You had the best part," said Joan, as if to console him, "driving down the Mediterranean coast."

"It was time for your turn, I suppose," said Thomas, "but I would have thought it would have made more sense for the drivers to take regular turns."

"It would, but there was no question of turns. How I eventually got into the driver's seat is a sorry tale. All the way through France, whenever we stopped for a break, we'd have a drink of the local wine. And whenever we stayed overnight we'd have more."

"There's nothing sorry about that," Thomas interrupted.

Richard ignored him and went on. "After two days travel, some of the group were taking advantage of the situation and were having one more for the road again and again. By the time we got to Spain, things had gone from bad to worse. At this village after Figueres, we ended up having an argument about getting going and I walked out of the bar in disgust after making my position quite clear. The Holborn was at the front of the four ambulances, and when I walked over to it, I was surprised to see that the keys had been left in the ignition. I jumped in, started the motor, and just sat there fuming. Soon the others came out of the bar. Fletcher jumped in beside me and the previous driver meekly got in the back with the other fellows without saying a word."

"I'd say he'd had one too many, and knew it," offered Thomas.

"Maybe he just felt guilty, or was scared that you might report him," added Joan.

"Anyway, you were right Joan, the drive down the coast to Valencia was spectacular, so different from England. The orange and olive groves, the vineyards and vegetable plots, the blue sea to the east and the ragged mountains to the west. It seemed like paradise after being shut in the back all the way through France."

3

THE ROAD TO MADRID

Huete staff meetings provided the opportunity to give reports and voice concerns. Sometimes a visitor, usually a political·commissar, would tell about the progress of the war, invariably in a spirit of morale-boosting optimism. Towards the end of one meeting in November, Nan Green said they had received a special request from Madrid for someone to broadcast to London about their experiences in the war.

"It is to encourage more volunteers of course," she said. "Dr. Hart and I have had a discussion about this and decided that Richard is the best person to go."

"Me!" he exclaimed. "Why me?"

"You've got a lot more to talk about than most of us," she beamed back at him, "and in any case, you're a good talker!"

"And so say all of us," chipped in Thomas, much to the amusement of all, particularly as he had the gift of the blarney himself.

"But I'll be tongue-tied in front of a microphone," pleaded Richard.

"No you won't. We've thought about that. Nurse Harrison will go with you and on the journey you can rehearse with her what you are going to say."

"I wonder whose idea that was," muttered Thomas. Joan cast him a chilling glance which only had the effect of eliciting from him a self-satisfied smile. Not what she had intended. If Nan Green had seen this exchange of expressions, she ignored it. Richard hadn't and his reluctance evaporated at the thought of going to Madrid with Joan. He admired her posh voice, her education. He thought she was everything he wasn't, yet she still gave him the time of day.

"They want you on Saturday," said Nan, cutting into his reverie. "Joan's Spanish will see you through the road blocks, and I'll arrange for the address and directions you need and the authorisations."

*   *   *

After a simple breakfast, they set off in one of the small ambulances. There had been a heavy frost overnight as was common on the Meseta, but as the sun rose higher it started disappearing on the east facing slopes. It remained below freezing for some time, as cold air had been sliding down from the heights, the Altos de Cabrejas, throughout the night. The landscape had a stark beauty that again made Richard think of the Pennines in Northumberland, but the colours were brighter and the edges sharper. Not here the regular rain that rounds the hills and dark clouds casting a gloomy light. They were travelling south from Huete on the dirt track to Carrascosa Del Campo where they would join the Cuenca to Tarancón road.

"It is about eighty miles to Madrid," said Joan, looking at a road map on her knee. "That gives us about three hours to sort out what you might say in your broadcast." Producing a small notebook, she continued, "Perhaps the best way of doing this is for me to ask you questions about where you have been and what you saw, and then we can decide what might be suitable to say in the broadcast."

"So you're going to be the censor," responded Richard, averting his attention from the road to grin at Joan.

"Well it wouldn't do for you to put your foot in it, because you might be broadcasting direct."

"Right then. What's your first question?"

"Let's start at the beginning. What happened when you got to Brigade headquarters at Albacete with your convoy of ambulances?"

"I was told to be ready to take the Holborn to the Jarama front the next day to join the Fifteenth Brigade. I don't know what happened to the other ambulances. I slept in the Holborn overnight, and in the morning this officer-type, who turned out to be Peter Kerrigan, came up to me as I was cleaning the windscreen and said, 'Are you ready?' And without waiting for an answer added, 'Let's go!' Ted Fletcher was with him. He went into the back and Kerrigan came into the front with me. Kerrigan told me he was on the Executive of the British Communist Party. That was easy for me to believe as he was an impressive figure; tall, dark and fit-looking. He had a strong Scottish accent."

"So Jarama was your baptism of fire?"

"More like baptism of blood." He was thinking of the terrible wounds of many of the Brigaders and Spanish comrades he had evacuated from the front.

"I can imagine, I saw the same on the Aragón front." Joan knew that the battle of Jarama had been a bloody affair with many hundreds of casualties on both the Republican and Fascist sides. And that the battle had been initiated by the Fascists, who had planned to cut the Madrid to Valencia road twenty-five miles southeast of the capital, knowing that the Republican government had moved to Valencia.

She knew that if the Fascists had been successful they would have severed land communication between the government and Madrid. The battle had started with a surprise attack, achieved by scouts from Franco's Moroccan army, the Moors, knifing Brigader sentries before dawn. The Jarama River was crossed and the main road cut. However, there had been a build up of Russian tanks and aircraft in the area before the attack and the Fascist advance was halted. They were driven back and forced to take up defensive positions. The Fifteenth Brigade had been heavily involved. Its British Battalion had been shelled and raked fiercely with machine-gun fire at what they called Suicide Hill. Battalion commanders Tom Wintringham and then Jock Cunningham had both been wounded. Fred Copeman took over. He also was wounded, taking some schrapnel but he stayed in command. Casualties in the ranks had more than halved the original battalion strength of six hundred. The Franco-Belgian and Abraham Lincoln Battalions had also suffered badly.

"What was it like when you got there?"

"The fighting was still going on and there were plenty of casualties to be dealt with, but the Fascists had lost their advantage."

"And who did you report to when you got there?"

"After I had dropped off Kerrigan and Fletcher, I was told to report to a Dr Minkoff, who was in charge of the Fifteenth Brigade medical services. He was a stern, solidly built Slav, and I got off on the wrong foot with him because I had thought that my ambulance would be mainly at the service of the British Battalion. He told me abruptly that I would be serving the entire Fifteenth Brigade: the Dimitrovs, the Lincolns, the Washingtons, the Mac Paps, not just the Brits. Of course, I had no idea that the Fifteenth Brigade was such a mix when

I arrived. Just imagine: Slavs, Americans, Canadians. Of course, there were Spanish comrades fighting there as well.

"I am just thinking," said Joan, scribbling in her notebook, "you should say something about how good it makes you feel being alongside comrades from all parts of the world who have come to save democracy from fascism."

"That sounds good!" exclaimed Richard, at last feeling that there was something definite that he was going to say. "I can add that we're not called the International Brigades for nothing!"

"They will like that."

Joan was pleased that he was getting into the spirit of things. By this time they were approaching Carrascosa Del Campo and they turned right when they reached the main road. Within a mile they were flagged down at a road block. The Spanish officer smiled when he saw their Brigader badges and checked their authorisation, and then he gave them the clenched fist salute and waved them on.

"I think he was pleased that you could speak the lingo," said Richard.

"It always helps. Anyway let's get back to it. What was the medical set-up like at Jarama?"

"I'm glad you asked that. When you suggested that I should talk about Brigaders coming from all over, it reminded me that there were two Australian nurses at Jarama. They were working day and night in the hospital at Colmenar de Oreja. It was there that I took the badly wounded, those who couldn't be patched up by the doctor in the lines or at the first aid post."

"I remember you mentioning them once when we were talking in the garage. I think you should say something about them. Can you remember their names?"

"Yes, one was called Fay and the other Una. That's right, Fay McFarlane and Una Wilson. They arrived in Spain with two other Australian nurses who were sent somewhere else. They told me a Spanish relief committee had been set up in Australia by trade unionists and some Labor Party people. They collected donations and called for volunteer nurses to help the Republican cause. The Australian government, being a lackey of the British government, tried to stop them but couldn't because they were non-combatants like us. Even the Labor Party didn't support them."

"Why was that?" queried Joan, knowing well that most British Labour Party people supported the Republican cause.

"They said half of the Party were Catholics, who were being told by the bishops that Franco was on God's side. The Party leaders thought that to take sides in the war would split the Party down the middle."

"So they sat on their hands."

"That's a good way of putting it," said Richard surprising himself at the momentary reversal of their roles. "But lots of trade union people put their hands up and they put their hands in their pockets as well. Funds were raised for their sea passage to Spain and for medical supplies to go with them. They said they set off from Sydney with quite a fanfare and were given receptions by unionists in all their ports of call in Australia. Let me see, that would have been Melbourne, Adelaide and Fremantle. After Fremantle, they would have crossed the Indian Ocean and Mediterranean to get here."

"How do you know all that?" queried Joan.

"Because I've been there," was the matter-of-fact reply. "I've sailed the same route but in the opposite direction. Only once, mind you."

Joan had been looking at the buildings as they passed through the small town of Alcazar Del Rey as he had said that. She turned suddenly to look at him. Now she realised why he was different from many of the other British Brigaders. His composure and self-reliance was borne of experiences long before Spain. Experiences of which she had just gained a glimmer. The pause in conversation caused Richard to turn his eyes from the road to meet hers. It was the first time that he entertained the suspicion that Joan did not just think of him as a fellow Brigader. But commonsense told him he was imagining things, she was posh and educated, and who was he but a Geordie driver.

"Well, back to Jarama, you still haven't told me much about the medical set up. What was the Colmenar hospital like?"

"Makeshift. A two storey building with a courtyard at the back and a garden at the front. I was told it had been a small local hospital before the war but not for surgery. So the operating theatre was in a kitchen and operations were done on the kitchen table. When I first got there, they just couldn't cope with the numbers of wounded. The rooms were crammed full with hardly room to move between the beds and stretchers. Some were just lying on the floor. It must have been awful for the nurses trying to look after those who could recover and comforting the dying at the same time. It was impossible."

He was gripping the wheel tightly and staring at the road ahead. Joan could see from the muscles working in his jaw that he was reliving his experiences.

"Once," he said, "I went into the courtyard and there were all these lads laid out like sardines in a can. They were covered in sleet. It was bitterly cold. Some looked dead but others were moaning and groaning." His head was moving from side to side as if surveying the courtyard afresh. Joan reached across and firmly gripped his knee. It was enough for him to switch from reliving to just telling the story. "I dashed back inside and I must have shouted 'What's going on out there?' at the Spanish medic, whose job was to sort out the wounded for surgery. He didn't know much English but he certainly knew why I was angry. He looked at me with the saddest of eyes and simply said 'no hope'. Their wounds were too severe. No chance of recovery. A quicker death would have been a blessing."

"That's often the case in war. I've been told more than once when I was on the Aragón front that the soldiers feared being badly wounded more than death itself. And also, that they believe that those who die for the cause are martyrs forever, particularly if they are volunteers."

"But, can't the badly wounded be martyrs as well?"

"No, you have to be killed for that. They might return as heroes, but that doesn't last. They often end up feeling encumbrances, bitter about the life they can no longer have."

"Only if the cause was lost would they feel bitter. If the cause was won they would remain proud of what they'd done."

*   *   *

By now they were approaching the outskirts of Tarancón where they would join the Madrid-Valencia road. They were again checked at a road block before being allowed onto the road. It had

26

to be protected at all costs. After all, that's what the battle of Jarama had been about.

A pensive mood prevailed in the ambulance for some time, until Joan broke the spell, declaring, "Don't talk about those conditions in the broadcast or they will think you are trying to discourage the lads, as you call them, from volunteering. Say what a great job the nurses are doing, including those two Australians."

"And including you, of course," he grinned.

"Don't you mention my name. I think all my family are on the other side. Anyway there must be some good things you can say about Jarama."

"Of course. We won the battle and drove them back. If we hadn't we wouldn't be on this road now."

"Well, be sure to say that," said Joan making further notes. "And what else can you say?"

Richard's mind roved over incidents which might be worth mentioning in his broadcast. That young lad, Raven, he thought, blowing his hand off with a grenade. Self-inflicted? Surely not. Not with a grenade. Anyway that won't do. That British driver shot dead while speeding through a road block by a French cavalryman. Odd really, he was going towards the front. Suicide? That won't do either. That young English lad, John Ball, with a serious leg wound, that he had dropped off at Colmenar and him having to wait his turn in the queue for treatment. Dead next day. There must have been more than a leg wound. No, I can't tell that one. That Spanish driver charged with sabotage for stalling a Russian lorry in the middle of the road to the front. Couldn't handle a crash gearbox. Richard smiled to himself.

"So what's amusing you?" said Joan, breaking into his thoughts.

"Did I ever tell you how I got my automatic?"

"What automatic?"

"It's here, under the seat."

She waited, thinking this should be interesting, since usually only officers carried automatics. Certainly not ambulance drivers.

"It all happened when I had to evacuate Merriman, the American Battalion commander, and a commissar called Springhall from the front. Merriman had a shoulder wound and Springhall had been hit in the face. Ted Fletcher went in the back with them. We were to go to a hospital further back than Colmenar, and when I stopped to check directions, Springhall became very agitated. He was thinking that if we strayed by accident into Fascist lines he'd be shot. Of course, he was right. Politicals are always targeted."

"I suppose that is because of their role in stiffening up the will to fight," broke in Joan. "And being communists. Franco calls them agents of Stalin."

Richard paused to pick up the threads of his tale. "When we eventually got to the hospital, Merriman was able to walk in, but Ted and I took Springhall in on a stretcher. Then when I took it back to the ambulance, I discovered his automatic under the pillow. I thought, he won't be needing it anymore, the state he was in, so I kept it."

"Brilliant. You tell that in Madrid and you'll probably get arrested for stealing a commissar's weapon."

"I was only telling it to you, Joan. After all I might need it to protect you."

The emphasis Richard put on 'you' gave Joan mixed feelings. She knew that he had meant what he had said and sensed that he was waiting for a response.

"Comradeship must be the only blessing of war," was not what he expected but gave him food for thought.

Some distance ahead a bridge loomed up. It was over the Río Tajo. There was a checkpoint before the bridge manned by Spanish soldiers. Richard slowed down to show his intent and stopped before the barrier. Joan passed the travel permit over to him as he wound down the window. Again the soldiers were friendly once they saw they were Brigaders. Joan, in her get-you-by Spanish, asked if there was anywhere in Fuentidueña de Tajo where they could get a drink. Yes, there's a bar on the right, came the answer. You will see the sign. This was communicated in mime as much as in words. They drove on, both glancing down at the river as they crossed the bridge. After a short distance they pulled over to stop at the bar. They were both relieved to get out of the cab and have a stretch after sitting so long. As Joan arched her back and swayed from the waist rhythmically, she noticed Richard watching her exercises with interest. She gave him a challenging look.

"I am not doing this for your benefit," she said, making him feel uncomfortable. And without waiting for a response, she walked into the bar. He recovered the keys from the ignition, and sat on a bench outside still feeling a bit uncomfortable. He didn't want Joan to get the wrong idea about his feelings towards her.

Inside, the bar was a dingy place. It hadn't had a coat of paint for years and the walls once white, were stained tobacco yellow. Behind the counter a moustachioed local was smoking and drinking red wine out of a small tumbler. Four other men were sitting around one of the small tables drinking and playing cards. They all looked up in surprise to see a young woman come into the bar, and apparently alone at that. Then realising that she was a Brigader, they broke into cheers and 'holas'.

"*Vino tinto o blanco*, red or white wine," offered the barman.

"*Tinto*," she responded, knowing they both preferred red wine. "*Dos por favor.*"

So she isn't alone thought the card players.

Joan took the drinks outside. "It's on the house. The barman insisted. I couldn't throw his generosity back in his face in front of his regulars."

"Well, you certainly got quite a welcome in there by the sound of things."

"Yes indeed. One of the men actually said, 'all Brigaders are my brothers.' I'm glad my Spanish was up to it. He was delighted that I had understood him."

Richard went to the cab and returned with some food they had packed for the trip back at Huete. *Chorizo* sausage, hard-boiled eggs, bread and a small jar of olive oil. Joan poured some of the oil onto a plate for dipping the bread. They sat with the food between them on the bench, enjoying the warm late autumn sunshine. A short distance down the road four boys were playing football with a tin can. The clatter and their display of skills provided a welcome distraction.

"Seeing them playing with that tin can reminds me of what some of the local kids used to get up to at Colmenar. They used to hunt around for unused bullets, and open them up for the gun powder.

When they had got enough, they'd make a trail with the powder along the road leading to an upturned empty tin can, just slightly tilted with a small stone. Under the can they would put a little heap of gun powder. They would put a match to the end of the trail and you can guess the rest. Watching Spanish comrades and Brigaders would join with the kids, whooping when the can flew up. It was a moment of fun for all of us."

"I think you should tell that story in the broadcast. It will make the people see that the Brigaders are fighting for real people. Volunteering for the preservation of democracy may appeal to the intellectuals, but volunteering to save children from the jackboot of fascism will appeal to ordinary decent people in Britain."

"I couldn't say what you just said."

"You don't have to say it that way, Richard, just tell the story and say how much you enjoy watching the tricks and games the Spanish children play when you're off duty."

He nodded to convey his acceptance of her advice, thinking she's making this broadcasting business a lot easier for me. "We'd better be off," he said, picking up the tumblers and taking them into the bar. His 'gracias' and 'adios' were returned in abundance along with 'camaradas' and 'hermanos'.

"What does hermanos mean Joan?"

"Brothers"

"You don't look much like a brother to me."

Joan smiled. "It's just a word they use to say that they regard you as family."

*   *   *

"I think we'll call in here on the way back, and next time we'll pay," said Richard, as he climbed into the driver's seat. Joan, already in the cab, was jotting down the tin can incident in her notebook. They were still some distance from Madrid. Fuentidueña was roughly the half way point on the trip. The wine gave Richard a glow and he was feeling relaxed and enjoying Joan's company. He was thinking that the last time he had felt like that was in the company of a Spanish lass who worked in the kitchen at the American hospital close to Madrid.

Joan noticed Richard seemed to be glowing and lost in thought. She wondered what he was thinking. "You look as if the wine's got to you," she broke in.

"It wasn't a bad drop. I was thinking how much better it was when I started taking some of the wounded, mostly Americans, to the Villa Paz hospital instead of Colmenar."

"Why was that?"

Richard waved his arm around in front of the windscreen, picturing the set up. "It was like a country estate with entrance gates and a long curving drive leading to this large mansion. The Americans had taken it over."

"It had probably belonged to some big landowner who had fled to the Fascists," interrupted Joan.

"The facilities there," he went on, "were far better than Colmenar. An American surgeon, Dr. Barsky, was in charge. He must have saved lots of lives. Everybody thought the world of him."

"You didn't miss chatting to the Australian nurses then? You must have missed them?"

Richard hadn't. His expression changed as he wondered if Joan knew the other reason why he had found Villa Paz a good place to take the wounded. He suspected she had heard something and the best thing he could do was come clean. At that point they were overtaken by what looked like a military staff car. Joan waved to the driver. It gave him time to think of how he could put it.

"One of the things I liked about Villa Paz was that I could usually get something to eat there. There was a Spanish lass in the kitchen who made a magnificent soup and if that wasn't on the go there was always something else. Juliana Bricio was her name. I really got to like her. Cupboard love I suppose," he added with a grin.

"I heard it was a bit more than that."

Richard had guessed right.

"I heard that she had a real gypsy look about her with long black hair and the flashing eyes of a flamenco dancer, and that you used to walk hand in hand with her in the hospital grounds."

Now he was embarrassed. The glow turned to a flush. He wished he hadn't said 'cupboard love,' it wasn't true and he'd been caught out. He'd seen Juliana regularly as the Jarama Front had stalemated and neither side saw benefit in attack. I would have married her, he thought, but it wouldn't have worked out. She only knew a few words of English and in any case the local girls were warned not to be taken in by the much admired Brigaders since most of them were married and had families. "Look, I didn't even kiss her," he pleaded, "so let's have no more of that. Anyway, when I got back from the Córdoba front she wasn't there anymore."

Joan reached across the cabin to ruffle his hair. "Poor thing," she said in mock sympathy, but inwardly she wondered if she was constructing for herself a false image of Richard as a knight in shining armour. He might just be like any other man of the working class that she had been brought up to regard with disdain. Feckless. She dismissed the thought, feeling ashamed that she had conceived it.

But he knew nothing of her fleeting misgivings. It was the first time Joan had ever touched him in an affectionate sort of way. The glow returned. At least I've got that off my chest, he thought and that attraction to Juliana got Elsie Dunn off my mind. I won't tell her that I was walking out with a lass in South Shields before I volunteered for Spain. It's over. She doesn't need to know. Not yet, he thought.

He slowed down as a convoy of lorries came towards them. The road was narrow and the surface was in a serious state of disrepair. The last thing he wanted was a collision caused by an unintended swerve by any of the oncoming vehicles some of which might not have seen him through the dust which the leading ones were kicking up. After they had passed and the road was clear ahead, Joan returned to the business in hand.

"So you went to the Córdoba front after Jarama?"

"Not straight away. The Holborn developed serious mechanical trouble that I couldn't fix myself, so I left it at Villa Paz for repair and was given a small Ford ambulance in exchange. It wasn't half so well equipped, but beggars can't be choosers. Later, I found out that after the Holborn had been repaired, the Americans turned it into a mobile dental clinic. A Doctor Kline was the travelling dentist, but I never met him. Did you?"

" No, but go on. There's nothing for the broadcast there."

"Next thing that happened I was told to drive these four chaps in a staff car to the French border. That was quite a treat for me. It was the middle of summer. First we had to go to Valencia and then there was that magnificent drive along the Mediterranean through Barcelona to the border and, of course, all the way back. Petrol, food, wine and accommodation all fixed up. I really enjoyed that. It was like a short holiday. Barcelona was thronging with people. Everyone seemed optimistic about the outcome of the war. I was never able to work out who my passengers really were. They could have been commissars, politicians or newspapermen. I didn't ask. It wasn't my place."

"So when you got back to Villa Paz, you were sent straight to the Córdoba front?"

"More or less. I think it was Minkoff's decision. He had already gone there to join the Eighty-sixth Brigade. I think I was supposed to go with him and possibly drive him there but then I was given the job of taking those chaps to the French border. Soon after I got back, a convoy of lorries was assembled and I was told to join it, still with a small American Ford ambulance like this one."

"Was there much action when you got there?"

"No. Just skirmishes. There had been fierce fighting the previous December, but it had become stalemated, just like Jarama. Of course, there was some work to be done as casualties were brought to the first aid post. Some had to be transferred to the hospital. Like

Villa Paz it was run by Americans. I was only there for a few days when Minkoff ordered me to take him to hospital. He was in a bad way. Malaria, I think it was. He was too ill to sit with me in the front, but he was up to putting himself onto a stretcher in the back. He told me he was to be taken to Murcia not the nearby American hospital. After an hour or so on the road we came to a railway station in the middle of nowhere, and I was flagged down. He was expected. Obviously arrangements had been made for him. He knew about it but why he hadn't told me I don't know. I was kept completely in the dark."

"That's the way the Russians work," said Joan

Richard was taken aback by the tone of certainty in her assertion. "Why do you say that?" he stuttered. "We're all Communists after all!"

"No, we're not. I'm not. The Anarchists are not. The Socialists are not. And there are lots of others who are simply for democracy. Just because you're against the Fascists doesn't make you a Communist. I know the Communists are in charge of recruiting the Brigaders in Britain and France and I know you joined the Party because you admired Minkoff so much that you thought it was the right thing to do."

"But you've just changed your tune. Now you're talking about Communists, but first you said Russians keep you in the dark. And Minkoff isn't a Russian."

"He's a Slav," retorted Joan, "it's the next best thing. In any case, what I'm getting at is who's pulling the strings."

There was a certain finality in her last statement. Richard shut up. He was confused. Obviously she's heard things that I haven't, he thought, as he changed gear to maintain speed on an uphill stretch of the road.

"I'm sorry for being so abrupt." said Joan, sensing his discomfort and realising that she was the cause of it. "I've heard some officers complaining about the way the Russians want to be in control. And I suppose they have the right to pull strings seeing that they're providing most of the aircraft, tanks and guns."

"You don't have to apologise to me. I'm just the driver."

"Oh no you're not. You're much more than that. There are not many people around with your knowledge of mechanics, and the way you reorganised the transport at Huete was magnificent. And the job you have been asked to do in Madrid is because you are not just a driver." She ruffled his hair again.

"Stop it, I'm driving." he exclaimed unconvincingly. Magnificent, he thought. No one's used that word about me before. He wondered.

"And what happened after you dropped off Minkoff?" asked Joan, changing back to the job in hand.

"I was told to report to Albacete for redeployment. I was only there two or three days and was sent to the Brunete front with two officers as passengers to join Walter's 35th Division. It included the Fifteenth Brigade and the British Battalion."

Joan grimaced. Brunete was where Richard was blown up. She had heard of the savagery of the fighting and of the enormous pressures on the medical rescue teams. And to make things worse the searing heat of the midsummer days without adequate water supplies and the chill of the nights. Those wounded had often lain in the open gagging for water, knowing that they wouldn't be rescued until nightfall, wondering if they would die from thirst or from their injuries. She knew of those torments from when she was working on the Aragón front and she knew that the fighting men had suffered even more at Brunete.

The battle had been a major Republican offensive to relieve pressure on besieged Madrid by cutting Fascist supply lines. 85,000 men supported by artillery, tanks and aircraft had been thrown into the offensive. The Republican armies had made early gains pushing the Fascists back as at that time the main enemy forces were engaged in northern Spain. However, Franco transferred forces to the Brunete front more rapidly than expected. And with the might of the German Condor Legion with its Heinkel bombers and its newly deployed Messerschmitt fighters, the Republican advance was halted. Air superiority had turned the tide. There had been large losses of life on both sides and very many casualties. Medical rescue had been stretched beyond the limits.

"How long were you there before you were injured?" asked Joan.

"Only five or six days. I can't remember exactly. It was chaotic. I wasn't counting the days just as I wasn't counting the trips between the first aid post and the transfer post. The field hospital was further back at a place called Villanueva de la Cañada. It was all go. Keeping the ambulance on the rutted road was hard enough but you also had to avoid all the military vehicles going to the front. Lorries, armoured cars, tanks, artillery - the lot. And there were lots of damaged vehicles on the side which had been hit. The jolting that the wounded got lying on the stretchers in the back must have been terrible. But what could you do? You just had to get them out if they were to have any chance at all. At any time a Fascist shell or bomb could take you out. You couldn't do anything about the shelling. If one had your name on it, that was that. With the bombing you usually got a warning. You might see the enemy aircraft yourself or you'd see vehicles rushing off the road and people diving for whatever cover they could find. The vehicles were the targets. They were bringing the supplies; munitions and men and food and water."

"Getting out of the ambulance to see what was going on didn't do you much good," said Joan, referring to the time when Richard was blown up.

"I think it was a bomb not a shell. There were certainly Heinkels about. It's strange really. After two or three days of action you can end up thinking nothing will happen to you. All I can remember about that incident was that there was a disturbance some way ahead. I was going back to the first aid post towards the front. I pulled over and, as you know, jumped out to have a better look. Watching silver bombs falling out of a clear blue sky has a special fascination. You seem to be able to block out the violence from the vision. But only for a few moments and only if it's happening some distance away. And before I spotted anything, 'whoosh'. I just felt a hot blast, then nothing."

"You were lucky not to get peppered with schrapnel. The ambulance must have protected you."

*   *   *

They both lapsed into silence as they approached the outskirts of the capital. Richard slowed down for another road block. They were held up only briefly as there were only two or three vehicles in front of them when they stopped. Now they could hear the crump of shells on the far side of the besieged city. '*No pasarán*, they shall not pass,' was not just an idle boast to the *madrileños*, the brave citizens of Madrid. The Fascists had not been able to penetrate the Republican defences. The city had already weathered twelve months of siege and every bomb and shell damaged building bore witness to it. But the people in the streets seemed to be in remarkably good spirits.

For a while they surveyed the scene until Joan burst in, "Well, about Brunete, I think the best thing for you to say is how quickly you your-self were rescued and evacuated to Huete where you were looked after by British doctors and nurses. That should reassure any would-be volunteers about how they are looked after if they are wounded."

As he continued to drive towards the city centre, Joan glanced over what she had written in her notebook and turning to a new page started writing more carefully than before. It didn't take long. "I'm not sure what is going to happen at this broadcast but I imagine that you will be interviewed. What I have just done is prepare a few questions which the interviewer might put to you. When we get there I will show the questions to whoever is going to do the job, and explain that we have been talking things over during the journey. The chances are that whoever it is will welcome the help. Of course, other questions might be asked, and you will just have to do your best."

"I'm glad you'll be with me," said Richard with a note of apprehension in his voice. "Tell you what, can you give me a separate list of questions and jot down some prompts?"

"Good idea." she wrote out the questions again and after discussing the prompts added them in. Question 1. What was the medical support like for the British Battalion at the Jarama front? First aid post.

40

Colmenar hospital. Australian nurses. Dr. Minkoff. Villa Paz hospital. Dr. Barsky. Holborn ambulance. And so on.

*   *   *

Although daylight was fading they had little difficulty finding the *calle* where the radio station was located. Nan Green's directions had worked well. Richard parked the ambulance and immobilised it. An old habit. They walked along the *calle* in one direction and then in the other until they spotted the sign they had been looking for. The guard at the door asked for identification. The Brigade service books and the papers from Nan Green did the job and they were escorted into the hallway.

"Where do we go from here? asked Richard, as much to himself as to Joan. No sooner had he spoken than a man came out into the hall from a side room and strode towards them.

"You must be the people from Huete here for the broadcast?"

"Yes," they replied almost in unison..

"Robert's my name," he said, in what Richard thought was an educated English accent. "I'll show you where it all happens. Follow me." He led them into a dimly lit basement. It was sparsely furnished with a number of chairs and two tables on one of which was a microphone. There were cables and other pieces of equipment lying around. It had a makeshift look about it. Emerging from the shadows of the room, a solidly-built man, bespectacled and balding, came towards them, eyeing Richard in a challenging manner. "So you're the ambulance driver who's been in the thick of it?"

A commissar, thought Richard. He could always pick them. "Since Jarama," was his brief reply.

"Where else then?"

"Córdoba and Brunete."

"Hmmm."

There followed a long pause. Joan thought the expression on the commissar's face suggested he was thinking about what this ambulance driver must have gone through on those battlefronts and how he might cope with the interview.

Eventually he smiled, but still spoke abruptly. "About this broadcast. There are just one or two basic rules. The British press and radio commentators refer to Franco's forces as Nationalists. You must call them Fascists or rebels."

" I couldn't agree more."

"And use the words comrades and brothers when you refer to the Republican forces and the volunteers of the International Brigades."

"On the way here," Joan broke in, "we have been discussing what Richard might say. I take it you will be conducting proceedings. Here are some questions he can readily answer." She held out two sheets torn from her notebook. The commissar was momentarily taken aback by being cut short, but given Joan's confident demeanour, he had little choice but to take them. He read through the questions carefully, trying to work out what answers might be given.

"I've got some prompts to help me out," interrupted Richard, handing over the jottings Joan had made for him. "We thought I should concentrate on saying how good the medical side of things is. How anyone wounded is treated quickly and evacuated if need be, and about there being volunteer doctors and nurses from all over. Britain, Europe, America, even Australia.

Glancing over the prompts, the commissar smiled again. "That fits the bill. You've saved me a job. And I like that question about the children and the gunpowder trick. Nothing like a bit of humour to get your message across. Back to business. You're not on until eight, so you have time to book in at your hotel, get something to eat and be back here at seven-thirty for rehearsals. Turn right as you leave the building and you'll soon find Calle Salud." As they got up to leave he added, "And no vino with that meal and remember, I can smell it from a mile away. I wasn't brought up a Methodist for nothing."

They walked briskly to the hotel reassured by the sight of *madrileños* going about their business despite the occasional sound of gunfire. To them it seemed too close for comfort. They booked in, had an omelette and coffee in the dining room and rushed back for the broadcast.

*   *   *

"The commissar seemed pleased with how it went," said Joan, "Strange he never introduced himself. Anyway, I thought you were just great."

"I couldn't have done it without you."

"We make a good team. I mean, the way we prepared together for the broadcast on the way here."

A team, he thought, what does she mean? But he didn't ask. The very thought of it added to his euphoria at having not only got over the ordeal of the broadcast but also being told he had done a good job. "Let's celebrate." he suggested. "There is a cafe along the street not far from the hotel."

Although it was fairly busy they found a table. Joan went up to the counter to find out what they had to offer in the way of food. She returned with two glasses of *vino tinto*. "I have opted for the *cocido madrileño*. It's a casserole, the local speciality. I feel a bit dehydrated and thought it would suit you too. It's one thing the Spanish do well. Anyway it will warm us up."

A dark haired waitress brought their meal to the table. She smiled at them as she arranged the plates. "Brigaders always welcome," she said.

"You speak English then?" asked Richard, above the clamour of Spanish.

"No," she replied, shaking her head, "but you English, I know."

"There must be something about us," said Joan with a laugh. "After all, we could be a score of nationalities."

" I think it was your posh accent."

They drank more wine than they should have, and although they thought not much notice had been taken of them, when they left for the hotel, they were warmly farewelled.

"Makes you feel appreciated," said Richard as they stepped into the cold, blacked-out street. "Back in England, they make you feel privileged to be served, unless they think you're important."

*   *   *

A few shells landed on the city as they were having an early breakfast. "They are just letting us know that they're still out there," said a man at the next table, as if to reassure them. By the way," he added, "my name is Carlos. I heard you speaking English and could not help myself. I was in London for two years trying to learn the language. It is good to get some practice." He was cut off by the crump of a shell falling not far from where they were. His smile was replaced by a grimace. "They think that they are terrorising us by shelling at irregular intervals so we will think it is never safe to go out."

"People don't seem to be terrorised. They seem to be confident of victory," observed Joan.

"Of course," the Spaniard went on, "they are proud of having stopped the Fascist assault on the city. This time last year, even the government thought that the city would fall, so it moved to Valencia. But Miaja produced a miracle, and everyone rallied to the barricades. The cry was *Madrid será la tumba del Fascismo*, Madrid will be the grave of fascism. And University City, where the battle still continues, has been the grave for countless Fascists."

It has also been the grave for countless Republicans as well, thought Joan. They had been less well equipped, but the Fascists found that it was almost impossible to advance through bomb shattered buildings against a resolute defence.

"But we would never have held out if it hadn't been for the International Brigades. They arrived just in time. With the government gone, morale was low, and we knew the Moors were coming. But when the Internationals marched through the streets on their way to the front, the change was beyond belief. Women wept and men too. Cries of '*Hermanos*' and '*Camaradas*' greeted them at every step. It was a scene I shall never forget."

Joan responded to this praise of the Brigades by reciting, seemingly more to herself than to anyone else, " Greater love hath no man than this, that a man lay down his life for his friends."

The Spaniard was visibly moved and drew his hand across his face in an effort to keep control. Richard was moved too, more because of the man's reaction than because of what Joan had said. "We'd better be going,' he said, trying to break away from thinking of the sacrifice his fellow Brigaders and their Spanish comrades in arms had made there. "Eat up." It hadn't been much. Bread. Olive oil. Sausage. But the coffee had been surprisingly good. However they had thoughtfully been provided with hard boiled eggs and some bread for their journey.

*   *   *

There was no shelling at the time they set off. The passage out of central Madrid and the suburbs was uneventful. Soon they were on the Valencia road. At the checkpoint on the outskirts of the city a queue of vehicles had built up, so that when they passed through it they found themselves in a stream of lorries and cars, much of it military.

"I don't like this," said Richard. "I like to see the road ahead. Convoys make easy targets from the air. It's much harder to hit a vehicle on its own." With that he pulled into the side at a point where there was a wide verge, stopped and waited for the convoy to get well ahead before getting underway again. Now feeling more relaxed he resolved to find out more about Joan's experiences in Spain. "You've heard all about my time here but you haven't told me much about what you've been up to since you arrived."

"There's not much to tell really. I didn't get here until the end of May and I was just doing theatre work in field hospitals."

"Is that all?" he replied with mock sarcasm. "Whereabouts were you?"

"About three weeks in Sierra Nevada, two weeks in Centio and the best part of a month on the Aragón Front. That was the worst. Lots of casualties. Quite a few died, one or two on the operating table. Some could have survived if we had got to them earlier. That has been a lesson of this war. Early intervention saves lives. By the time you get to see some of them, they can have lost so much blood they don't have a chance. Now they have started giving blood transfusions even in the front lines, if they can. Remember you telling me about a Canadian doctor you saw putting what you thought were bottles of blood in a stream? Well I told Tudor Hart about that and he said you had guessed right. His name was Bethune. He has been a pioneer in blood transfusion and has set up a mobile transfusion service. Now, lots of lives are being saved that would have been lost before."

Richard didn't respond to that for a while, his thoughts switching to individuals he had rescued and had later died. Perhaps if they had been given blood..... Who knows? But he had learnt not to dwell on what might have been. It gets you nowhere. You've just got to get on with the job. With that resolved he returned to Joan's experiences. "That's good news. I suppose your Aragón hospital must have been a bit like Colmenar?"

"Oh, it was not as bad as that. We were doing the attacking and after we captured Belchite, the front became stalemated. Then I was transferred to Huete."

"You must have gained a lot of experience in those hospitals."

"Sadly, medical knowledge and experience do benefit from war. You learn quickly from taking risks to save people. You do things you wouldn't get away with in peacetime."

They both fell silent as they looked out at the wintry landscape of the Meseta. After a long lull in the conversation, Joan broke in, "My experiences on the Aragón front make me realise what those Australian nurses must have had to put up with at Jarama. You made them sound like real heroines in your broadcast. Proper Florence Nightingales. Let's hope that anyone hearing what you said will think that if they were prepared to come from the other side of the earth to support the cause, then surely they themselves should do something."

"Let's hope some will think that way. After all, that was the point of talking about them."

Joan changed the subject. "Fuentidueña is not far off now. We said we would go back to that bar and offer drinks all round."

" I think we will have to get in quick."

Over the next rise Fuentidueña came into view. They slowed down and pulled over in front of the bar. This time they went in together and were greeted warmly by the owner and those customers who recognised them from the previous day. Joan called for drinks all round and would brook no refusal. They all laughed at her determination and one called a toast to the Brigaders when all glasses were filled. Joan explained to them that Richard had made a broadcast to London to encourage more to join the Brigades. One man who was somewhat better dressed than the others asked, "Why Richard?" Joan thought for a moment, then said, "Because he was at

Jarama and Brunete." The man took a deep breath and rolled his eyes. They all fell silent.

"Tell them I was only driving an ambulance," said Richard. "Don't make me out to be a hero." She told them what he had just said.

A second round of drinks was called by one of the customers and the atmosphere became convivial again. When they left, the bar emptied on to the road with them and they were sent off with shouts of '*Bravo*', '*Hermanos*', and '*Camaradas*'.

✳   ✳   ✳

"We had better have this food while we are travelling," said Joan, opening up the package they had been given at the hotel in Madrid. "It would have been impossible to start eating it in the bar with all the fuss they were making. What I love about the Spanish is that they are so much more open and welcoming than English people."

"Obviously you have never been up north," exclaimed Richard indignantly.

As they travelled along, she shared the food between them. "You had better open your mouth for these bits of egg, they are falling apart."

He laughed but did as he was told. "I think you're enjoying treating me like an infant."

"You don't seem to be complaining," said Joan, smiling broadly.

After they had passed through Tarancón, she broached a new subject. "Things are winding down now at Huete. Most of the convalescents are to be returned to their battalions. Tudor Hart's heard of plans for a big Republican offensive, and they want all units back to full strength. We will all have to be redeployed."

"We can't do much about that."

"We can. The two of us can work as an ambulance team. It was Tudor Hart's idea. He said that with my theatre experience I could save lives giving first aid to the seriously wounded at the front, increasing their chances of survival. And he thinks highly of you after what you did for the transport. He thinks we would make a good team."

Richard was taken aback by this suggestion. Team, he thought, team. Just the two of us working an ambulance. "You said we made a good team, after the broadcast," he exclaimed suddenly. Then just as suddenly he blurted out, "So you came to Madrid with me just to try me out, to see if we could work together."

"Well that was Tudor Hart's idea as well."

"So do I match up?" he asked with some indignation.

"It is not like that. It's a question of compatibility. We will not only be working together, we will be living together. In the ambulance, that is."

"But you haven't answered my question."

"Yes I have. We make a good team and I knew that long before I said it in Madrid."

"I thought I was taking you for a ride, but you've taken me for one," he said, grinning at his own pun.

"So we are a team then?," she said, half question, half statement. She reached across and put her hand on his shoulder and left it there.

He nodded, his grin widening. He had never felt better.

4

LEAVING HUETE

When they entered the hospital common room they were greeted warmly with 'Here they come', 'How did it go?', and 'How's Madrid?'

"Judging by your expressions, it looks as if it went well," said Tudor Hart, raising his voice above the others.

They gave all the news, taking it in turns. They both talked of the warm greetings they got from their Spanish comrades everywhere; at road blocks, in the bar at Fuentidueña and in the streets of Madrid.

"That's good," said Nan Green, "they obviously saw you were Brigaders. The *madrileños* know only too well that if the Brigaders hadn't arrived in the nick of time, they would now be under the jackboot of fascism."

"They're well aware of that, which is perhaps why they seemed in remarkably good spirits despite the bomb damage. At least that's the impression I got," added Joan.

"And the broadcast went well?" inquired Tudor Hart.

Joan said they had taken Nan's advice and had spent the journey rehearsing which of Richard's experiences he should talk about, and that the announcer in the radio station was more or less happy to keep to the script they had prepared,

"Sounds like good teamwork to me," responded Tudor Hart approvingly, "and does the team carry on?"

Nan knew what he meant. The others didn't. That word again, thought Richard.

"Yes," answered Joan, "but we'll need a bigger ambulance if we're going to be really effective. Richard thinks he might be able to get one at Villa Paz. He left his big Bedford there in June for repairs and wants to see if there is one still there that he might be able to exchange for one of our smaller Fords. If there is, at least he has a good case for an exchange."

Tudor Hart agreed to the proposal and said he would provide the authorisation.

*　　　*　　　*

Early next morning Richard set off alone to Villa Paz. Much of the route was the same as the journey to Madrid. The American hospital had been established close to Madrid to serve both the Madrid and the Jarama fronts. Being east of the city it was well out of the range of Fascist artillery and in any case it would have been unlikely to have been targeted as it was a former Royal summer residence. He had plenty to occupy his thoughts as he drove along paying little attention to the vastness of the Meseta. Most of all he was just hoping he would be in luck.

He could barely contain his anxiety as he drove through the gateway of the estate which housed the hospital. Undeterred by the rules, he sped up the curving drive to the place around the back where he knew ambulances not in use would be parked. Immediately he saw what he had hoped for; the distinctive shape of a Bedford. Closer inspection revealed it was the Wales, one of the original four he had come to Spain with. It looked in fairly good condition. Now for the difficult part he thought, persuading the administration to swap it for the Ford. If I can get Barsky to agree, it will work. He had known Dr. Barsky since Jarama after he had started regularly taking mainly wounded Americans to Villa Paz because its surgical facilities were far superior to those at Colmenar and because it was American.

Barsky is in his office, he was told on inquiring. Good, thought Richard, I can get him on his own and he won't be distracted. At least I hope not. The office door was slightly open and he knocked on it tentatively so as to attract Barsky's attention without startling him.

"Richard, come in. I haven't seen you for a while. Still at Huete? What can I do for you?"

"Yes I'm still there but that's going to change. I'm going back to front-line ambulance work with one of the nurses who's used to theatre work. Dr. Hart thinks that she will be able to patch up the seriously wounded quickly, before complications set in."

"That's good if she's up to it. Obviously Tudor Hart thinks she is. She must be something special. I can't count how many times I have been dealing with a case and wished I'd been able to get to him an hour or so before. But what's it got to do with me?"

Richard told him how he had left his original Bedford ambulance at Villa Paz for repairs and picked up a small Ford as a replacement, and that now he was looking for a Bedford because its size made it more suitable for the way they planned to work.

"Sounds like you're setting up a mobile hospital," beamed Barsky. "Well we do have one of those English ambulances. Just wait here. I'll check with transport to see if it's available." He returned a few minutes later. "That's O.K." he said, "but you will have to leave the one you came with."

Richard was much relieved. Barsky could see that and he was also pleased himself at being able to help what he thought was an innovative project. He smiled openly. "An ambulance with a built-in theatre nurse, now that's really something. Before you go, try the kitchen. You still look as if you need a good meal." Richard thanked him again and left for the kitchen. He hardly needed the invite and he certainly knew where it was.

The feel of the Bedford was quite different from the Ford, but he quickly adjusted to it, which was hardly surprising. Elated with his success, he could not find praise enough to heap on Barsky. A real gentleman, he thought. The way he treated you was so personal. Telling me to go and have a feed, and him a surgeon. I've never met a surgeon like him before. What a mix the Brigades have thrown together. Joan and me. That's an unlikely mix.

*   *   *

The journey back to Huete passed in a trance. He parked the ambulance in the garage and went in search of Joan. She was attending a patient in the intensive care ward. Although he caught her attention, he had to wait for her to finish the procedure. She had sensed his impatience and that he was bursting to tell her something. It was written on his face and in his body language.

"I've got something to show you," he exclaimed. "Come on."

Joan had difficulty keeping up with him. She had been taught that nurses never run. Running means panic, the matron at Bart's had repeatedly said and walking purposefully gives you time to think and conveys authority. She followed him across the courtyard to the side-door of the converted chapel. She had already realised that it had to be an ambulance but was still surprised to see that it was one of the big Bedfords with 'Donated by the people of Wales' inscribed on the side.

"A gift from the Welsh miners," said Richard, noticing her reading the inscription, "and from Dr. Barsky."

"More like a gift from God. It is just what we need. That storage space over the top of the cab will hold plenty of blankets and spare stretchers. Let us have a look at the business end."

Joan's business end was different from his. The rear doors opened easily, and Joan's mouth fell. "What a mess. No wonder the transport at Villa Paz let you have it. The interior just about needs rebuilding. It has really been knocked about in the nine months it's been here."

"But it's mechanically sound. It just needs a good service."

The *tendencia* had come into the garage to see who was about and joined in the inspection of the vehicle. He was obviously not well and looked thinner than ever. " 'Tis the inside that's the problem. 'Tis," confirmed Thomas in his distinctive brogue. "There's a man in the town who can fix that. There's nothing he can't do. But he'll need clear instructions. I'll try to get all the materials you need for the job."

They stood around the back, discussing the best layout for the interior, Joan saying what she wanted, the others playing devil's advocate. Finally, they agreed that on the left side double bunks should be built to carry two stretcher cases, and on the other side a wide bench for the sitting wounded which could, if required, support a canvas stretcher as could the floor space in the centre. It was a flexible arrangement. The ambulance could accommodate either four stretcher cases or two stretcher cases with four sitting on the bench, and even more if some sat on the floor.

"We'll go and see the carpenter first thing in the morning," said Thomas between coughs. "The ambulance will have to be left with him for some time."

*　　*　　*

Next morning, Thomas introduced them to José, who had already been pleased to do a few jobs for the hospital. The challenge of refitting the interior appealed to him. Thomas explained that Joan was in charge of the specifications. Then he and Richard walked back through the town to the hospital leaving Joan to explain her requirements. She wanted lockers under the bottom bunk and the bench and also an overhead locker above the bench. In addition she wanted a let-down table just inside the door on the bench side, where water could be boiled on a Primus stove for sterilising instruments or for making tea, coffee or a simple meal. She explained that when they went into front-line service, the ambulance would be their home. José pulled a face at that. A better-you -than-me expression. Then he asked mischievously, "Who will sleep in the top bunk?"

They both laughed. "No-one," she responded. "The top bunk will be left empty."

Joan monitored the refit on a daily basis, becoming quite friendly with José and his wife and family. Like all the Spanish people she had come into contact with, she was warmly welcomed as a Brigader. José said he had heard about what was going on in Nazi Germany and didn't want a fascist Spain. Once the children had got over their shyness, they would ask Joan questions and giggle at her replies in broken Spanish.

In the meantime, Thomas had managed to obtain thin mattresses for the bottom bunk and the bench and lengths of oilcloth to cover them and the top bunk as well.

"That's important. Blood can be wiped off the oilcloth coverings at the end of a trip or at the end of the day, so that new cases are not presented with the gory evidence of those that had gone before them," she explained to José. "Being put in a clean ambulance is very reassuring to a wounded comrade."

Once the refit had been completed, Richard brought the ambulance back into the garage for a thorough mechanical service. He also gathered together and stowed tools and spares for emergencies. The hospital was able to provide Joan with blankets and medical supplies; bandages, sutures for stitching up wounds, hypodermic syringes, anaesthetics and painkillers.

By the time the ambulance was ready, many of the hospital patients had been returned to the front-lines. Nan Green was also to be transferred and so she was pleased to give Joan as many medical supplies as she could carry in the lockers. In addition, Thomas had provided kerosene and meths for the stove, and food supplies such as sugar, tea, coffee, tins of beef and condensed milk, chick peas, beans and olive oil. A considerable quantity of water was also carried in leather bottles, which they were able to squeeze into whatever spaces were left in the lockers.

*　　*　　*

It had taken more than two weeks to prepare the ambulance. Now Richard and Joan were ready for service with the Fifteenth Brigade. They had been assigned to the Teruel front. However, Tudor Hart was also leaving Huete and wanted them to take him to Valencia before they reported to the Brigade. It was a bitterly cold December day when they left. They all made their farewells to the remaining staff with whom they had worked for several months; Nan Green, Thomas Kerr and the local Spanish staff. "*Adiós. Hasta luego,*" were Joan's poignant parting words; poignant because in such a war, it could only be hoped that they would meet again. Joan sat between Richard and Tudor Hart in the cab as they set off in the direction of Cuenca. A brooding atmosphere took hold, which puzzled Richard. He had been looking forward to the time when he could return to the job he had volunteered to do; working the ambulance at the front. And with Joan, for whom he had gained a strong affection, things couldn't be better. It's Tudor Hart, he thought, glancing across, observing his grim expression as he surveyed the snow covered heights of the Altos de Cabrejos. Perhaps it was leaving the hospital he was in charge of. Perhaps he's worried about what awaits him in Valencia. Joan was every bit as much aware of the mood, but a different interpretation was passing through her mind.. Not long after she had arrived in Huete, Tudor Hart had expressed that his regard for her went beyond the professional. Joan had been flattered but made it quite clear that his feelings were not reciprocated. Respecting him for his skill as a surgeon was very different from becoming involved in an intimate relationship. Now she realised that his feeling had persisted, and that he now suspected that her feelings for Richard went beyond the professional. Perhaps he was rueing the day he had suggested that they worked together as an ambulance team.

Eventually Tudor Hart broke the silence. "You won't have heard much of Teruel. It's not a large town but it is a provincial centre. The Spanish army under the command of Lister and Heredia have completely surrounded the Fascist garrison there. It was a brilliant surprise attack under cover of heavy snow. Without giving any artillery warning, our Spanish comrades occupied all the heights around the city. The Fascists drew back their outlying forces into the city itself, and now they are defending it building by building. The International Brigades have not been committed yet. They are being held in reserve. The government wants this to be a Spanish victory, to let the world know that Franco can be beaten by a Spanish Republican army."

"But he is sure to counter attack, like he did at Brunete," said Richard.

"Yes, that is expected, and you will have plenty to do once you report to medical services at Teruel."

"Sounds like we will be in the thick of it," added Joan.

As they approached Cuenca the spectacular scenery provided a temporary release. Above them towered the crags of the Río Jucar and Río Huécar gorges, with the ancient town perched precariously on the spur between the converging rivers. Some houses even seemed to hang over the edge of the gorges, looking as if they were about to plunge into the river below.

At Motilla del Palancar they joined the Madrid-Valencia road where an irregular stream of lorries and cars and at one point a number of tanks, almost certainly Russian, were going in the direction of Madrid. Conversation was sparse. They were all lost in their own thoughts. When they passed through the last check point before Valencia they found themselves in a different world. The greenness of the *huertas*, the orange groves and vineyards, abruptly replaced the winter bleakness of the Meseta and its stark snow-capped sierras. They farewelled Tudor Hart in the city at a place of his choosing and drove north out of the city in the direction of Sagunto.

5

TERUEL

Once clear of the city, they stopped on the side of the road for a short break to have a stretch and something to eat and drink. Richard and got the Primus going and soon they were enjoying coffee with their *chorizo* and olive oil dipped bread. To the east beyond the orange groves, vineyards and vegetable plots, the blue Mediterranean stretched to the horizon. Sitting on a low bank, the warmth of the winter sun and the view dispelled the gloom they had both felt during the journey to Valencia.

"Tudor Hart was keen on me. Wanted me to go to China with him to work for the Red Army," said Joan abruptly.

So that was it, thought Richard. Tudor Hart had fallen for her but she had rejected him, and him a surgeon. Nurses are supposed to dream of marrying a doctor let alone a surgeon, he puzzled. Then an explanation struck him. She doesn't need to be a social climber. She's already up there. That's why she's so confident. So sure of herself. Able to talk easily with anyone. Officers, ordinary soldiers, even ambulance drivers. He smiled at his own self-deprecatory humour and at his belief that he had at last got something of Joan's measure.

She noticed, wondering if he was thinking about what she had said concerning Tudor Hart and herself. And if he was, why the smile. But she didn't ask.

"We had better be off if we're going to make Teruel before nightfall," was all she said.

At Sagunto they purchased some fresh vegetables and fruit. Then they left the coastal road and turned inland. There was now a lot of military traffic on the road; tanks, cars, motorcyles and lorries loaded with munitions and other supplies heading for the front and mainly empty lorries coming the other way. The road followed the fertile valley of the Río Palancia for thirty miles but after passing through the *pueblos*, small towns, of Segorbe and Jérica, it climbed steeply up onto the Meseta. Being more lightly loaded, they were able to overtake a military convoy carrying heavy equipment and supplies. Now almost the entire landscape was blanketed in snow; the sierras, the pine forests of the upper slopes, the terraces lower down and the valley flats. Only the steepest crags and terrace walls exposed themselves. And the road, the vital supply line to the front had been kept clear. It was a scene of stunning beauty.

"Reminds me of the moors. The Pennines in winter," said Richard, breaking the spell.

"I have seen nothing like it. It makes me think of Siberia, not that I have ever been there. I've just seen pictures."

As they approached Teruel, they came to a *pueblo* where military vehicles were being assembled. It looked chaotic and Richard didn't want to get caught up in the middle of it, as it was starting to get dark.

"I think it would make sense if we found somewhere to park for the night and report for duty in the morning," said Joan.

"I was thinking the same. Let's not get caught up with this lot." He turned onto a track which led off to the right and continued down it for about a mile. The track then dipped into a small gully. There was a place under some trees where they were able to pull in. He jumped out, lifted the bonnet and threw a blanket over the motor to keep it warm for as long as possible. Also he attached a piece of cardboard in front of the radiator for the same purpose. Joan went into the back, put the small table down and lit the stove to boil some water. She scooped two mugs full of *garbanzos*, chickpeas, which she already had soaking in a container, and tipped them into the only pan they possessed. A chopped up onion and *chorizo* were added to it along with water once the kettle had boiled.

"That smells good," said Richard, joining her in the back. He closed the doors and lit the small hurricane lamp. It cast a warming glow in the interior. Joan used the rest of the hot water to make a weak coffee.

"Dinner will take a while," she said. "You can't rush *garbanzos* or you will break your teeth on them."

"It'll be a long night. It's damn cold out there. I'll have to start the motor up now and then to stop it freezing up. I'll put a hot water bottle on top of the water pump as well."

Joan smiled as she held him in a steady gaze thinking, thank God I'm with someone who knows what he's about. He wasn't sure what to make of the look but it did make him wonder what Joan's feelings really were towards him. He knew what his were well enough. But I'm just a driver, he thought.

After they had eaten and cleaned away there was nothing else to do but to rug up and try to get some rest if not sleep. They had plenty of blankets, so there was no problem in keeping warm. Joan chose the bottom bunk and Richard the bench so that he could easily get out to check on the motor and fire up the Primus for the hot water bottle.

"Tell me how you came to go to that school you went to." asked Joan. "It was a reform school wasn't it?"

And so began a cathartic ritual which went on almost every night they were together in the ambulance. It was invariably Richard telling his story. Joan insisted that she had little to tell, certainly little of interest. 'There's nothing worth telling about a private girls boarding school, stupid rules, terrible teachers and bitching girls, and hospital nursing was in many ways more of the same. Discipline, uniforms and doing what was right or proper, especially proper,' was her usual response.

"Well, I got into trouble. I got mixed up with lads two or three years older than me. We broke into places and messed things up."

"How old were you?"

"Nine when it all started. Dad died when I was eight, and I just got into bad company. I don't know why it all happened. Maybe because I was the youngest and was trying to show off to the others."

"Did you miss your dad?"

"I suppose I did, but I was surrounded by family, my mother and my brother and sisters, aunts and uncles, and my grandparents. After dad died I often stayed with them. When I stayed with granny I used to run all the messages. I had to go to different shops for different things to get the best or the cheapest. Sausages, tripe and black pudding from Billy Blytheman's. Groceries, butter, cheese and flour from the Co-op and cabbage and rhubarb from the allotments. You didn't have to shop for fish. Hawkers used to trundle round the back streets with baskets of herrings in handcarts. Real cheap they were."

"You are making me feel hungry again. So what was the cause of your father's death?"

"I'm not sure. He was wounded in the Dardanelles in Turkey, but now I think that it was the coal dust down the mine that got to him. He was a putter, loading coal all the time. He was only twenty-seven when he died."

"Your mother must have been devastated to become a young widow with a family to look after all by herself."

"I didn't think about that. I was only a youngster. I had my brother Cecil and my sisters Mary and Ellen and all the relatives. Mam wasn't the only one. The Great War must have made plenty of young widows."

Joan was quiet after that remark and soon after it she fell asleep. He waited for a while and then went out to run the motor, which he did three or four times that night. She slept through it all.

*   *   *

Next morning they awoke to the distant sounds of war. Joan made coffee and they dunked stale bread into it for breakfast. Careful not to spin the wheels, Richard manoeuvred the Wales back onto the track and within minutes they were back in the *pueblo* on the main Teruel road. The concentration of military vehicles of the night before was gone. A sign told them it was La Puebla de Valverde. It

65

was as yet unscathed by the nearby war as if protected by the Sierra de Camarena which straddled the landscape between it and Teruel. The morning sun paled by a thin layer of cloud endowed the snow-covered landscape with a strange luminosity, making the village with its angular buildings seem a discordant intruder.

"They've cleared the road for us," he said, picking up speed as they left La Puebla behind. Joan made no immediate response as she stared in the direction of the Sierra.

"It's like Antarctica."

"Yesterday you said Siberia. Make your mind up."

At Venta del Puente the road snaked through the Sierra and finally they were pulled in at a checkpoint on the outskirts of Teruel. Joan got out of the cab and explained in her improving Spanish that they were to report to the Fifteenth Brigade. She wanted to know where it was. The soldier went to consult an officer who came back with him to the ambulance. The officer greeted her warmly and told her that only Spanish divisions were fighting in Teruel, that soon the rebel garrison would fall and that the International Brigades were in reserve and many miles away. He insisted that their medical support was desperately needed to support the Spanish divisions. He added with a smile that they could wait for their Brigade to join them rather than them join it. That said, giving no time for dissent, he directed them to a first aid post some distance from the town.

It was only mid-morning when they arrived at the post and already there were wounded Spanish comrades waiting for treatment and evacuation. Joan did what she could for those in urgent need of attention in the ambulance; injecting, cleaning, stitching and dressing. Once they had a full ambulance they would drive some distance to a designated transfer post and drop them off to be taken to a field hospital further from the front.

It was bitterly cold in the daytime and the nights were even worse with icy winds swirling around the *muelas*, molars, the flat-topped steep-sided heights which surrounded Teruel. In the deep snow comrades often died overnight to be found in the morning as rigid as logs. But recovering the dead was not ambulance work. That was for recovering the living. Many of the Spanish soldiers they had to deal with were not wounded but were suffering from frost bite. They would straggle down to the first aid post from the heights in ones and twos, the worst cases sometimes supported by comrades who were themselves afflicted by the frost but not so severely. For the worst cases, amputation was the only treatment and they knew it. The ambulance and its blankets provided only temporary shelter, as once dropped off at the transfer post, they were out in the open again waiting their turn for further evacuation. And that wasn't always by ambulance. They were in short supply and often open lorries had to be used for both wounded and frost bite cases.

The first day at the front had been exhausting for them. Darkness fell early as it was midwinter and as the cold intensified, gunfire fell away. Richard parked the ambulance for the long night with the bonnet away from the wind. It would help a bit. They both went in the back, washed the bloodstains off the stretcher covers and got the Primus going for a hot drink and a meal. It was cosy in the back with the soft light of the hurricane lamp and the roar of the stove. The interior wasn't exactly warm, but they were out of the biting winds. And after they had eaten the best place to be was bed.

"What was it like for a boy living in South Shields?" asked Joan. She knew he didn't need much encouraging.

"I need time to think about that. I don't know where to start."

"Well, start with where you lived."

"I'm not sure I want to. You living in such a posh house and all that."

"Go on, no one's responsible for what they are born into."

"Alright then," he said, conjuring up a picture of his house and home. At first, he spoke in a monotone, almost like a child reciting a poem just learnt.

"Stevenson Street, South Shields. That was the address. It was at the end of a row of terrace houses. We just had the upstairs. Downstairs was a small corner shop selling things like paraffin, candles, soap and the like. The family that ran the shop lived behind it. Our family had two big rooms, and a small scullery where you did the cooking and washing up. One of the big rooms was the bedroom with two double beds, one for mam and dad and the other for the rest of us. Me and my brother slept at one end and my sisters at the other. In winter mam would warm a plate in the fireside oven, cover it with a pillow case and warm the bed up for us. The other room did for everything. There was a cast-iron range with a coal fire and an oven off the side, a big wooden table where we all had our meals and dad had an armchair he used to slump into when he came back from the pit. Stairs led down to the front door which opened straight onto a stone flagged footpath and cobbled street. At the back of the house was an attached wash house and a small flagged yard leading to the lane. There was a gate at the bottom of the yard and on one side of it were two brick coalhouses one for us and the other for downstairs. On the other side of it there was a dry toilet which we shared with downstairs. It was whitewashed inside and kept immaculate. That was the word. There was always a bucket of ashes and a shovel at the ready. The cartman came down the lane and shovelled out the waste through the hatch, and the coalman delivered coal in the same way. Waste out, coal in."

Joan could tell from Richard's changing pace and tone that he was back at home. But it was almost twenty years since he had lived there and it wasn't easy for him turning pictures into words. "I can see it all myself." she said reassuringly, suspecting that he was uncomfortable describing his humble circumstances to someone he thought of as having had a privileged childhood. "You described it so well I could really picture it."

"But you didn't hear the sounds or see the sights around where we lived."

"Well I will not be able to unless you tell me about them, so go on."

And he did, now haltingly, as if to savour each memory. "The sounds. Well, you knew who was about from the sounds. The clatter of the coalman was different from that of the cartman. The solitary clogs of the lamplighter and the knocker-upper, and the massed clogs of the miners leaving home and coming back. The calls of the fishmonger, the scissorman and the gypsies selling pegs. The clatter of the iron hoops run by the lads over the flags and cobbles. The sounds of wash houses working overtime on Mondays all up and down the lanes. And afterwards, the flapping in the wind of sheets and shirts overhead across the backs. Then the splashing sounds of mothers and children having their weekly bath before emptying out the washtub.

Joan's hmmm told him she was still listening.

"And the sights. Dad back from the pit, covered in coal dust. I'd help him get his clogs off and mam would prepare his bath in front of the fire. It was a big zinc thing. Sometimes we used it too. Sometimes we went to the pit head and took the miners' lamps from them and hung them up in their proper places. Other times we went to the slaughterhouse to watch the action, hoping we would be given a blown up pig's bladder to play football with. We watched aunts make clippy mats from rags and mothers whitening their stone doorsteps to make them the most welcoming in the street. All of us made decorations from newspapers at Christmas time to festoon the main room while the women prepared the Christmas pudding and mince pies. Shouting up the chimney for Father Christmas and always finding my sock full of sweets and an orange and an apple in the morning. I don't know where to stop. There were the cliffs, the beach, the jetty, the lighthouse, fishing boats, colliers, cargo ships and battleships. I fell down the cliff when I was six and nearly scalped myself. I was in hospital for a week."

"Sounds a lot less boring than my childhood." said Joan, "Nothing much happened that I can remember. Not like your South Shields which sounds like it was teeming with life. The best part of my childhood was in the books I read."

He couldn't think of what to say to that but after a long pause he said, "The motor needs a run."

*　　　*　　　*

When he returned she was already asleep. It had been a long day.

The next two or three days passed quickly with countless trips between the first aid post and the transfer post with wounded or frostbitten Spanish soldiers. Despite all Joan's ministrations, death sometimes came in the ambulance. Head wounds and chest wounds the usual culprits. Disfigurements were the worst to cope with. But they had to keep going. When they picked up food at an army field kitchen, they were told time and again that the fighting in the streets of Teruel was still going on. As if they couldn't hear it! Apparently the Fascists were well entrenched in the seminary and convents on the south-west edge of the town. They were all massive stone buildings perched at the top of the steep slopes of the Río Turia valley. Their position commanded the valley and the *muelas* to the west. Consequently the assault was a slow process. Fascist resistance was stubborn. Franco had got the message through to his garrison commander Rey d' Harcourt to fight on as relief forces were being dispatched. And so the bloody struggle went on from December 1st to January 8th. But there was a respite, at least there was for Richard and Joan.

6

THE BLIZZARD

On New Year's Day, returning late from the transfer post where they had just dropped off four badly wounded and frostbitten Spanish comrades, the light snowfall turned into a blizzard as biting winds swept down from the *muelas*. Richard slowed down to a snail's pace, wipers thrashing to clear the windscreen. Eventually he found what he was looking for, a place where he could pull the ambulance well off the road and face it downwind. He breathed a sigh of relief, now confident that no vehicle trying to cope with the blizzard could possibly hit them. Richard grabbed the thick blanket from under the seat and jumped out, lifted the bonnet and covered the motor. By the time he had the bonnet down, Joan was in the back priming the stove for a nightcap. They were both exhausted physically and emotionally from the number of trips they had made that day. Conversation was sparse and after they had cleaned up they bunked down.

When dawn broke they were stunned by an eerie silence. No rifle cracks, no chatter of machine guns, no explosions.

"Something's happened," said Richard, opening up the back of the ambulance as the back windows had snowed up. The blizzard showed no signs of stopping. It denied visibility yet they both stared out at it as if expecting at any moment to be able to see through it. "I think we'll take the day off," he said in a jocular manner, closing the doors quickly so as to let no more snow in. "Let's brew up."

"You never finished telling me about the bad things you did as a young boy." Joan was determined that if the blizzard was to shut them off physically from the war, they should shut their minds to it as well.

He felt he had no choice but to tell the truth even though he thought Joan might think less of him when she knew it. They were both sitting together on the bench side-by-side, feet propped up on the edge of the lower bunk. Drawing comfort from the warm mug of tea he was clasping, he began. "I got into bother four times. First time, three or four of us were coming back home from the beach through the allotments. We broke into a shed and found scores of eggs in drawers. It was an incubator. Someone started throwing them about, and we all got into it, making a real mess of the place. We were found out and had to go to court, but I was let off."

"Being your first time I suppose."

"Yes. Then I got pally with a lad called Chris Gardner. He was older than me. Anyway, we broke into a warehouse full of plaster castings and started throwing them around, and breaking a lot of them. I don't know how we were found out but we were, and again I had to go to court. Gardner got off because it was his first time, but I was given six strokes of the birch."

"And you only a little boy."

He ignored her sympathy and went on. "I was taken down to the cells. I was dreading what was going to happen to me so much that when the court officer came along I almost felt relieved. I just wanted to get it over with. He told me to strip, then marched me down the corridor between all the cells into a small room." He paused. "I don't know if I want to go on with this."

"I can take it if you can. I want to know what you went through." She reached across and ruffled his hair. The break and the reassurance helped.

"In the middle of the room was a table and a chair and I was told to use the chair to get up onto the table. Then I was told to put my arms over the shoulders of a burly policeman who had his back to the table. He grabbed my wrists and bent forward. The court officer said I should count the strokes out loud. By the time I got to six I was shouting at the top of my voice, even though there were other people in the room. Just the pain!" Tears welled in his eyes as he relived the experience.

Joan hugged him. "I'm sorry. I'm sorry it happened and I'm sorry I put you through that."

"That's all right. I forgive you," he said with a weak smile. "I couldn't sit down for days, but you wouldn't believe it, when I was back in the cell, the court officer brought me a mug of steaming hot tea. I can still taste that cuppa. It made me feel a lot better."

"And after that you got into more trouble?" said Joan in disbelief.

"I can't believe it myself, but I still stayed pally with Chris Gardner and we both got birched for the next offence. You know, now I can't even remember what that was for anyway. I volunteered to go first. I didn't want to hear him howling. The last time I got into trouble, we had palled up with an older lad, Donald Telford. He was nineteen and I was only ten. We tried to steal a boat anchored in the Tyne but couldn't start the motor, so we had to row back to the bank in the dinghy we'd pinched. The plan had been to go to France. It was Telford's idea. Well, we were spotted, and all three of us ended up in court. Gardner was birched again, Telford was jailed for three months, and I ended up being sent to the Abbots Memorial School in Gateshead for six years."

"I find it hard to believe they would do that, and you only ten years old."

"It was the fourth time I'd been before the court and they must have decided that my mother couldn't control me. My uncle Mac thought that I needed discipline and as far as I know he was the one who insisted that I should be sent to the school. Most of the family were upset about it, blamed him, and some of them never spoke to him again."

"And how did they treat you there? What was it like?"

"Hang on. I'd better start her up. You brew up again and I'll use what's left for the hot water bottle."

*   *   *

The blizzard was still raging outside, but he persevered with starting up the motor, a routine he would carry out throughout the winter whenever the ambulance was stationary for any length of time. The first signs of frost on the windscreen or back windows would activate him. He knew well that if the block froze the ambulance would be useless with chances of repair almost non-existent. They would be stranded and he could be charged with negligence. When he returned Joan handed him the hot water bottle. He went back and carefully placed it under the blanket.

75

"Looks like it's really settled in," he said shutting out the blizzard with a slam.

"Get your coffee."

Richard wrapped his numbed fingers around the mug, then took a swig. "That's great," he said. The condensed milk had made the coffee more than palatable.

Joan was propped up at the far end of the bench, also mug in hand. "Come on. Sit down. You were going to tell me about that school. What was it like? Was it a big place?"

"I was only ten when I went there, and to me it was a huge place. Three storeys with a courtyard. Dormitories on the top floor and workshops, classrooms, a gym and a recreation room on the other floors."

"Workshops! Did they make you work like prisoners?"

"Oh no. Nothing like that. They were trying to teach us trade skills. That's what they called them. There was a carpentry shop, a metal workshop with a lathe and a blacksmith's furnace where we would temper chisels and the like, a cobbler's, where we mended our shoes and a tailor's shop where we made vests, shorts and shirts. Of course, there were classrooms as well where we had ordinary lessons."

"Sounds like you learnt a lot. But was it all work and no play?"

"They usually kept us busy, even when we weren't having lessons but there was play."

"The devil finds work for idle hands," said Joan, adopting a moralistic tone. They both laughed. She raised her eyebrows inquisitively, meaning 'go on'.

"We played football and cricket on the cinder patch which was part of the school and I got into the teams. I also got into the gym team. I was good at that, vaulting over horses and the like. Don't laugh, but we had a dancing team and when I first went there, being among the youngest, I was dressed up as one of the girls in the team. Then there was the school band. I played the tenor horn and later the bass horn."

"You talk a lot about teams. Who did you play against?"

"Oh, we played against the local schools and we often thrashed them because we were better trained. We had all the time in the world to practise because we didn't go home."

Joan's 'hmmm' gave recognition to Richard's sudden change of tone.

But he went on quickly as if to escape the thought of having been deprived of everyday family life. "We went camping every summer for two weeks at Walkworth Castle. I always looked forward to that. We used to give band and gym displays in the village and play the locals at cricket. Once I scored forty-nine. I was proud of that. What was best was just getting out of school. Normally that only happened when we were competing against someone, or when we went all scrubbed up to Sunday morning church. We all sat on one side. Always the same side. No one ever spoke to us." There was that change of tone again.

"You must have been able to get home sometimes," Joan insisted.

"That's right. But only on Sundays and I wasn't allowed to stay overnight. I couldn't get away before ten in the morning and I had to be back before six. The train went as far as South Shields, and from there I had to walk across the fields to Cleadon where my mother had moved to. After about a couple of hours at home I had to set off back. And it was even harder for my mother to come to see me. I just about stopped going home eventually. You had commitments to teams and the like."

"It sounds as if you weren't ill-treated or abused while you were there."

"Never. The headmaster, Mr Barlow, wouldn't allow it. If you did something really bad, you would be sent to him. But that didn't happen often. Everyone was strict with us, but they were always very fair."

"Surely there must have been times when boys did the wrong thing, like bullying or swearing or maybe stealing? After all, none of you were there because you were angels."

Richard thought about that. After a while he said, "The reason we didn't run amok which all of us must have done to be sent there, was because of the way they organised us. We were all put in groups of about ten with one older boy being the leader. When it came to doing the chores, each group would have a different job, and these would be done in turn so you didn't get stuck with the same one. Some jobs were easier than others, and you'd groan when it was your turn to clean out the lavatories."

"But that does not explain what stopped you from doing something wrong."

"The whole group got punished, that's what. The last thing you wanted was for the lads in your group to be blaming you for landing them with extra chores, or worse still, having special treats taken away from you, like a piece of fruit cake or an apple."

Joan nodded trying to imagine what Richard had been through. "What was the food like?"

"As good as we got at home. Lots of bread and dripping. Mugs of cocoa in winter and tea in summer. Never coffee. Porridge in winter, stewed rhubarb in summer. Cabbage, carrots, potatoes and lots of stews with dumplings. We didn't starve but we were always hungry."

"Not surprising, seeing how busy you were kept."

"The place started changing after a couple of years. They stopped sending young lads there and as the older ones left, the numbers fell. There were about a hundred and fifty when I arrived but only about sixty or so when I left."

"Was that better? The smaller numbers I mean."

"Not really. As the numbers went down, some of the teachers were taken away and some of the workshops were shut up. Also it was harder to make up teams, and we lost the bandmaster. Oswald, a senior boy, took over that job. In my last year there I didn't do much more than look after the boiler room, keeping the boiler stoked so that the washrooms and kitchen had plenty of hot water."

"Did anyone leave before their time was up?"

"Not really. But I did. Oh yes, I remember, there was one lad, McVittie. He was let go because his parents were migrating to Australia. He sent me a postcard of the ship he went on. The Themistocles, it was. Such an unusual name that I remembered it. Mr. Barlow saw the card and told me how to say it. It's a Greek name. Someone famous. Anyway, I missed McVittie. I never found out how he got on down-under." After a pause he added, "That

79

reminds me, I wonder what happened to those Australian nurses who were at Jarama. They did have funny accents."

Joan laughed. "And what do you think they thought of yours?"

*   *   *

Joan opened one of the small tins of French beef they carried for a midday meal. She served it on a bed of rice with red peppers they had bought in Sagunto. Flavoured with wild thyme, it was a meal far superior to what they usually picked up at the army canteens.

"Good tucker," said Richard with a grin, relishing every mouthful. "Especially with a drop of vino."

"What did you say? Tucker. Where did you get that from?" queried Joan.

"From my sailing days. It's what they call food in Australia. When we went ashore, we'd be asked in the pubs if we wanted any tucker to go with the drinks."

"How much of Australia did you see then?"

"Not much really. We only called in at three or four ports to pick up a full cargo of wheat and then went to China. The ship was the Dalblair, general cargo. We'd picked up coal at Mombasa for some place in Arabia, then returned to Mombasa to pick up more coal. We off-loaded that at Durban, then sailed light ship to Australia, right round the southern side. Nothing to the south of us but Antarctica."

"Did you see any icebergs?"

"We weren't that far South. Never more than forty degrees. The first place we called in at in Australia was a port with two long jetties. It was called Wallaroo. It was a long way up a deep gulf. When we went ashore, leaving the locals to hump the wheat bags, I remember it was scorching hot. Up and down the main street, the shops all had big wide verandahs so you could walk up and down in the shade. And the houses had verandahs too. People used to sit out on them and call out to passers-by. The strangest thing though was that the pubs didn't open at night. They closed at six o'clock. We found this out when a few of us went for a drink. Anyway, as it happened, the publican came out and asked if we were from the ship. As if it wasn't obvious! Then he took us in through a side door to an empty room and told us to keep the noise down. He couldn't serve the locals, he said. It was the law. And it would only take one of them to report him to the police for serving the sailors to get him into trouble. So there we were, sitting on the floor with our backs to the wall, grateful for the drink despite the discomfort. The publican explained that the law was meant to keep the men at home in the evening."

"Well, we have the laws in England just the same," said Joan. "They close in the afternoon. Fellows would stay in the pubs all day if they didn't close up. But I think Australia has it right. Men should be with their families in the evenings, doing things with them." She realised what she had just said, so to distract him from thinking about his lost family life, she quickly asked, "And where else did you go in Australia?"

"Two or three places, but I can't remember the names. Port Kembla was one of them. On the east coast. Not a bit like Wallaroo which was very flat. Behind the town were rugged hills covered in gum trees. Bluey green in colour. Often you'd get the smell of the gums if the breeze was in the right direction, and particularly after it had been raining. It was a refreshing sort of smell, like pines, only different." He paused, gathering his thoughts. "After that we went to China."

China sounded so exotic to Joan, making her think she'd been nowhere.

"Yes, straight to Shanghai where we off-loaded the wheat. Then we sailed north again through the Yellow Sea. I remember as we sailed north seeing the lights of Port Arthur to starboard. We picked up a load of coal at a small port not far from the city of Chinchow. It was the northern winter by then. Bitterly cold. The wind was coming off the land and everything was covered in snow. We dropped the coal at ports along the coast as far south as Shanghai and kept returning for more. We did that for three months. Once we went up the Yangtze as far as Hankow. We had a very slow passage going up. While we were anchored there we saw one poor devil executed, beheaded by the authorities. I suppose he was a criminal, but fancy doing it in public."

"*Pour encourager les autres.*"

"What did you say?"

"It's a famous French saying. The French mistress at school used to use it if one of the girls asked why she was being punished for some trivial misdemeanour. It means they executed him in public as a warning to others about what would happen to them if they turned to crime."

"Sounds like you think they did the right thing."

"Nonsense." Joan was indignant. "I don't believe in capital punishment. I am not a nurse for nothing."

Richard felt uncomfortable. "Let's brew up," he said to relieve the tension. He briefly opened the back of the ambulance although sure of what he would see. They both stared out at the still falling snow. It separated them from the reality of the war they were in. They both drew comfort from that although it was unspoken.

"Did you go ashore much?" she asked.

"Oh, we're back in China are we?" He gathered his recollections. "Once in port we weren't allowed to handle the cargo. There were plenty of Chinese to do that. They loaded the coal into baskets and carried it on or off on their backs. Scores of them. There were markets everywhere selling just about everything. Silks were popular purchases for foreign crew to buy for taking home for headscarves or whatever. I never bought much. I didn't earn much. Shoes and dungarees were cheap, and I bought those once or twice. When we went ashore we always felt safe. We were never hassled like happens in Arab markets. The Chinese we had dealings with were very courteous. Almost too much so. Just before we left China, we saw Japanese troops invading just north of Shanghai at a place called Wusong. There were British, French and American navy ships anchored in the area. They just looked on. Didn't do a thing."

"It's called non-intervention, Richard. It seems that the so-called democracies are hell-bent on appeasing militarists. What was it all about?"

"Well, I was told that the Japanese had just taken over Manchuria in Northern China and set up an independent state there, even installing a puppet emperor. Anti-Japanese riots against this broke out all over China, but Japan invaded where it did to protect the large number of Japanese who lived in Shanghai. At least, that was what they said. The Japs, I mean."

"Was that invasion the reason you left China?"

"Oh, no. We had to be replaced by Chinese crew. Only the officers and engineers stayed on. The Chinese came on board with their rice steamers and food supplies. I got the impression that they would eat better than we did. They looked really organised the way they set themselves up with their rice steamers on the deck. So we were paid off in Shanghai, said farewell to the Dalblair officers and returned to Europe as passengers on an Italian ship. It docked at Genoa, and from there we got home by rail, except for the Channel, of course. I had been away more than twelve months."

"That was one big trip," exclaimed Joan. "You were away a year and you saw more than I have seen in my entire life!"

"You almost make it sound as though I was lucky. We had to put up with a lot. It was even colder than here, which reminds me, I'd better do the motor."

*   *   *

While Richard was out, Joan started wondering why he had turned to seafaring; why after years at the reform school he had not been glad to just go back home; why he had even stopped going home after Sunday church services while he was still at the school. Team commitments he'd said. Not letting the team down. It dawned on her that the school had become his home, its activities and relationships replacing those of family life. Home had become no longer home.

"How did you get into that life? On the ships I mean," she asked after he had settled back in.

"From the school."

"Just like that?"

"Well, yes. Mr. Barlow, the headmaster, was involved. He called me into his office to discuss what I was going to do when I left the school. He knew that my education there had come to a dead end. I was just looking after the boilers as I said before. I was head monitor by then and I think he wanted to make sure I got a job, which wasn't easy at that time as the miners were on strike and all the colliers were laid up in the Tyne. I told him I wanted to go into the Royal Navy as a cadet, but he thought that wasn't a good idea. 'You've missed a lot of home life in the last five years,' he said. 'If it's the sea you want, the merchant navy would be better. You'd be staying at home between ships. It would be a more normal life.' I agreed with him because I knew he really cared about me. In a way, he'd replaced my dad."

"I find it really amazing, Richard, just how many good people were at that school. I was thinking while you were out that it became a home away from home for you. Enough of what I think. What happened next?"

"The headmaster's clerk took me round the shipping offices in Newcastle. I was hoping to get an apprenticeship on a ship called the Sheaf Mount, but that was overseas at the time and was ordered not to return to England because it would have been tied up like the others. Instead, I was taken on by the Sheaf Arrow as an ordinary seaman. It was just a small collier. It was able to sail because it wasn't picking up any cargo in England. I remember the day well, the fifth of November 1926. I was woken up at six in the morning, went down to the kitchen, made myself a cup of cocoa and two thick slices of bread and dripping, picked up my kitbag, walked to Gateshead railway station and caught the train to Sunderland where the ship was docked.

A foreign seaman welcomed me aboard when I shouted up to him that I was new crew. His name was Jacob Bosetti. He was the watchman looking after the ship while it was in port. So up the gangway I went and he showed me the poop and then took me down into the foc'sle. It smelt of wet clothing and smoke. It was warm enough as a bogey fire was kept going, but I felt hemmed in. I was to get used to living in small spaces. He gave me a top bunk and showed me a locker where I could store my personal things. I hadn't much. My kitbag just contained seaman's clothing which the school had provided. Oilskins, thick jerseys, woollen socks, seaboots and a sou'wester. After chatting for a while, he told me I'd better get down to the shipping office to sign on and join the union and after that I should go to the chandler's and get my donkey's breakfast."

"Your what?"

Richard laughed. He was lying on the bench, having got weary of just sitting on it. "It's a palliase filled with straw. That was your mattress. No pillow. Just two heavy blankets was all you had."

"And what was the first voyage like?"

"It turned out to be a baptism of fire, as they say. When I got back to the ship, I was called on deck to help the other seamen batten down the hatches in preparation for setting sail. It was getting dark when we set off, so we had to hoist the navigation lights. It was raining cats and dogs. We were going to Rotterdam to pick up a cargo of coke. The trip there was fine. The holds were filled with coke, and because it was a light cargo, the gunnels were built up by lashing planks of timber to the stanchions, so that extra coke could be carried on the deck. There must have been two feet of coke on it. Well, on the trip back across the North Sea, a storm sprang up out of nowhere. As the bow buried into the waves huge amounts of seawater were thrown up onto the deck and the coke soaked it all up, making the ship top heavy. It started listing. 'All hands on deck,' went up the cry. 'Release the gunnel boards'. I was below at the time and got ready as quick as I could, tucking my oilskin trousers into my sea boots. Just as I was about to jump onto the coke to help the others, the ship's Russian carpenter grabbed me by the collar and hauled me back to the bridge. There, protected from the spray by the cowl, I watched the seamen release the planks allowing the deck cargo to slide into the depths. The ship steadied. The carpenter pointed at my boots with a smile. I looked at his, then I realised; you don't tuck your oilskins in. That explained why I was paddling around with my boots full of water. I was glad to get ashore when we docked at Dunston. I learnt a lot on that first trip!"

"I'm sure you did. And when you were only fifteen," said Joan, as if she was talking to herself, trying to take it all in. "Did you go anywhere else in that ship?"

"Oh, yes. One trip to Huelva in southern Spain to pick up a cargo of cork. That was a light cargo too, so again we carried it on the deck as well. But we didn't have any problems. Even though we had to go through the Bay of Biscay which is notorious for storms and rough seas, it was calm enough for us. The last trip on that ship for me, was to Bergen in Norway, and then into the Baltic, to Kemi in Finland and Danzig in Poland, picking up cargoes of timber. I was paid up in July 1927. Eight months that was."

Richard was quiet now, as if he had said enough.

"Well I think it's time to have something to eat," said Joan

"That'll be great. I'll go and start her up again."

With that, he opened the back, jumped into deep snow and slammed the door behind him. It was still coming down.

* * *

"So you went to sea straight from the school without going home first?"

Richard recognised that Joan was finding that hard to believe.

"There wasn't time. The Sheaf Arrow was leaving but I used to go home between voyages," was the almost apologetic response. " My mother had remarried while I was still at the school. My step-father is a nice fellow and we get on well. He found work as a carpenter at Catterick army camp for a while, and I went there to stay with them after the Sheaf Arrow. I did a few odd jobs to help him while I was there. He thought I should try to get an apprenticeship in a trade. Most of my aunts and uncles were still living in and around South Shields, so I went back there for Christmas. At the Labour Exchange they suggested that I should apply for one of the merchant navy training courses at Gravesend on the Thames. I did and was accepted on the seamanship course. It lasted 6 months. They worked you really hard."

"What happened after that?"

"I went back to sea as an ordinary seaman, the bottom rung, on a Canadian mail ship, the Beaverburn. It was a fast ship. The food and the accommodation was really good. I shared a cabin with three other seamen. I did four Atlantic trips. One to Montreal and three to St. Johns. It was real luxury after the Sheaf Arrow, but there wasn't much to do; not much chance to practise the skills I'd learnt on the course. Just keeping watch was the main job."

"And you wanted to be doing things," nodded Joan with a half smile.

"The truth is that general cargo ships are the hardest work and tankers are the easiest. The oil is just piped on and off. Again, keeping watch is the main job. I did a lot of voyages on tankers. Let me think. There was the Malistan, the Silverfield, the British Inventor, British Prestige and the British Sergeant. Most of the trips were to the Persian Gulf, through the Suez Canal. Abadan was the place, right at the head of the Gulf. We went there ten or eleven times. One of the other places I went to on the tankers was to Tuapse. That's in Russia on the Black Sea. We all called it Topsy."

"That's typical," said Joan with a laugh. "During the Great War, British soldiers in France, changed all the French names they found hard to pronounce. The town Ypres, they called Wipers. Sorry, I interrupted you. You were saying there were other places you went to in the tankers."

Buoyed by Joan's continuing interest he carried on.

"Los Angeles was the only other place. We were going to go round the Horn, but it was too rough, so we went through the Magellan Straits. Both ways."

"You certainly got around. You must have seen a lot of things."

"Not so much on the tankers, because you don't go into a proper port. You just tie up at an oil terminal." Much to Joan's surprise Richard then broke into song.

"I joined the navy
To see the world
And what did I see?
Nothing but sea."

She laughed heartily at his music hall impression. "It can't have been as bad as that."

"No. But the general cargo ships were the best. There was a lot more to do on board and you went right into the ports. You went ashore, and met some of the locals. Occasionally, you got very friendly with some of them. I remember going in the middle of winter on the Maid of Andros to the Russian port of Odessa on the Black Sea. We got there in January. That would have been 1931. It was bitterly cold and the ship was frozen in for a while. We were in port for more than a week and went ashore all the time. The locals were very friendly, even the guards. Everyone wore oversized overcoats and their feet bound up in felt cloths looked huge. They looked clumsy and comical to us. But of course, we didn't laugh at them. We were invited to the opera theatre which was in a fine building with marble staircases. The opera was about Chinese capitalists forcing young girls into prostitution to make money. The evils of capitalism, that was the message. Another place we went to was the Youth Club where I became very friendly with a chap who worked for the Central Telegraph. He spoke English very well and could write in

English too. Victor Ludkovski he was called. He told me that messages that he had taken indicated that the Maid of Andros was in financial trouble. I liked him so much that I even thought of jumping ship and living in Russia, but he told me that being unable to speak Russian, I wouldn't survive. Anyway, we wrote to each other for three or four years. It was probably the only time I was sorry to leave port for the voyage home. Victor was on the wharf to see us off. The return trip was terrible. It even started off badly. I was standing on the foc'sle head and there was a seaman below coiling in the ropes. Well he started shouting about something, then his voice got weaker and weaker. Someone looked down into the hold to see what was happening, and there he was, buried under coils of rope. So it all had to be brought back up on deck to release him. He wasn't injured but he couldn't stand up. Drunk on vodka!"

"He wasn't used to it," offered Joan.

"Oh, he was used to it alright. He just didn't know when to stop."

"You said it was a bad trip."

"We ran into a lot of foul weather. We made for shelter on the east coast of Sicily until the storm abated. Then we ran into another storm which was even worse. It's the only time I've experienced oil being poured overboard to calm the sea. We were hardly moving at the time, but it did work."

"I suppose that's a pretty desperate measure. The captain must have thought the ship was at risk."

"I suppose he must but no one panicked. That gets you nowhere. We just got on with the job. We put in at Malta for shelter and for bunkers as we were running out of steaming coal and we even sought shelter off the Tunisian coast for a while. It was a good job that the wheat was well stowed with bagged layers on top of the loose wheat. If it hadn't been and the cargo had shifted, we'd have been done for in that weather. I can tell you we were all glad when we docked at Liverpool. We'd been away for four months."

"I'm surprised you ever went to sea again after that."

"Well, I was certainly glad to get home and rest up for four or five weeks. Then I signed on on the Dalblair. That was the Australia and China voyage I told you about."

"I'm just amazed that you would do that. On second thoughts, I'm not."

They were both sitting on the bench now, feet perched up on the lower bunk opposite. It was the most comfortable position in the ambulance short of lying down. Richard gave Joan a puzzled look wondering how she could change her mind so quickly. And what did it mean? Her direct smile disarmed him. She knows me better than I know myself, he thought. "Make a cuppa, and I'll do the usual."

With that, he jumped out of the back into the still swirling snow

*   *   *

"I think I heard some explosions," he said, clambering back in. "Perhaps they've been fighting all the time we've been here, taking advantage of the blizzard grounding the Fascist planes."

"You're probably right, but I would have thought we would have heard something. Still, we're stuck here until the snow stops and the road gets cleared. So where else did you go, sailor?" Joan made it sound as if she would now believe almost anything he said.

"Haven't you heard enough?" was his reply as he sipped his still hot tea.

Joan responded with a hint of disappointment, "Surely you haven't come to the end yet? I mean your adventures at sea."

"Adventures! Is that what you call them? They weren't voyages of discovery."

"Maybe not to you, but they are to me, in more ways than one," pronounced Joan enigmatically. She saw from his expression that he was uncertain what she meant by 'in more ways than one'. But he didn't seek an explanation. He was simply pleased that Joan wanted to hear more, pleased that he wasn't boring her.

"Apart from sailing on the Cookham from the Tyne to Bilbao where we left the ship for scrap, and coming back on the train through France, there was only one more adventure as you call them, and that was to America."

" Bilbao, Bilbao," repeated Joan. "Isn't that near Guernica?"

"Yes. Guernica is inland. It's about thirty miles away."

They lapsed into silence, both thinking of what had happened there on a market day the previous April. They had both seen the bomb-blasted streets of Madrid together in November and could well imagine the devastation that had been inflicted on an entire town by the Heinkel bombers of the German Condor Legion.

"I thought Belchite was bad," said Joan, breaking the tension, "but Guernica was a surprise attack, and most of those killed were civilians. It was no accident. It was market day. They knew the town would be crowded."

"Let's hope Teruel has fallen by the time we dig ourselves out." He thought that referring to what he hoped would be a Republican victory would lift their sombre mood. It did.

"Now let's get back to your last grand adventure"

Richard grinned. "It turned out to be more than I bargained for. I signed on on the Synington Court in South Shields May 1934 it was. Our destination was Portland, Oregon, on the west coast of America where we were to pick up a cargo of timber. We went out light ship, but because it was a long voyage, we carried extra bunkers in number two hold. That was a lot cheaper than putting into a foreign port to buy coal which had been shipped there in the first place. It was a good ship. Very orderly. The firemen worked four hours on and eight off, and the seamen's watches were four on, four off. There was plenty of deck work. Splicing wire and rope. Stitching canvas hatch covers. Painting wherever it was needed, caulking the deck seams, and in good weather holy-stoning the decks."

"Now I know where the expression 'keeping it ship-shape' comes from," interrupted Joan, "but it is usually applied to houses, offices, or shops. After all, you would always keep a ship, ship-shape."

"Yes, but some are kept better than others, and even on the best run ships, accidents can happen. The Synington Court proved that."

"So what did happen?"

"Well, when the coal in the main bunker ran low, we had to transfer coal to it from the number two hold so that the boilers could still be fed directly. The problem was that the hatch to the number two was lower than the main bunker. So what we had to do was to build up a platform around the hatch with bags of coal. Then using the derrick, we could winch up baskets of coal which seamen were filling in the hold below and swing them across to the main bunker for spilling. Unfortunately, when number two hold was almost empty, one of the bags of coal on which a seaman was standing gave way and he fell straight down the hatch. Broke his neck and his back. Killed instantly. We all felt bad about it. He was a popular chap. First Class seaman. He'd been at sea all his life. That night, all stitched up in a canvas bag, after a prayer from the captain, we slid his body off a hatch cover into the sea."

"It must have been like losing someone from your company at the front."

"In a way. But you expect death in war. You know someone will cop it. But not on a ship."

They were both quiet for a while. They had both already seen plenty of death and dying in Spain, Joan at Belchite, and Richard at Jarama and Brunete. And Teruel's blizzard was only a respite.

"You know, if it wasn't for your stories, I think I would go mad in this ambulance. Visions of you on the deck of a ship in the middle of the Atlantic is a wonderful antidote for claustrophobia."

Encouraged by that he went on. "Nothing out of the ordinary happened for the rest of the voyage and when we got to Portland there was a strike on the docks. Portland's not on the coast by the way, it's a long way up the Columbia River. The scenery is really spectacular. Mountains and forests everywhere. When we docked, union people came on board to explain what it was all about and to persuade us to join the strike. I agreed with their arguments and walked off the ship in support. I had to find somewhere to stay, which wasn't difficult. I soon found a boarding house. A chap who was staying there, Jack Moulds, took me with him to see one of his friends. His name was Bill. He was part Cherokee Indian I was told. The next door neighbour was there as well. Joe Hindley. I really took to him. He was very friendly, with a great sense of humour. He invited me next door to meet his wife and family. There was Ethel who was sixteen and a lad of about twelve. They were all really friendly and before I left, Joe invited me to come and stay with them. Of course, I was delighted. Much better than where I was. So I moved in and just about became one of the family. Mrs. Hindley treated me like a son and Joe used to go with me to the union offices every day to find out what was going on with the strike. I joined the union and gave myself a false name as I had no right to be living in America. Richard Daniel Buck. Someone told me if the police stopped me and asked me where I was from, I should say New England. The point was I had a funny accent to them and West Coasters all thought New Englanders had funny accents. Also, I should say I was a fisherman and went out on the dories.

The strike continued and there was a lot of unemployment as the depression was on. Joe was hard up, but he did get some money from two or three other houses he owned, but most of his tenants were in arrears. Lots of people were on food vouchers. Cherokee Bill, next door, told us he was going to put a deposit on an old car and go fruit picking in the Yakima Valley. I didn't like doing nothing and asked if I could go with him. He was happy with that, and I did have a bit of cash to help out from the Synington Court."

"So now you really did become an illegal immigrant."

"That's right, I suppose."

No supposing about it, thought Joan, but said no more, not wanting to distract him further.

"We filled the back of the car with some food supplies, mostly cans, blankets and stuff, and set off up the Columbia Valley. Bill drove as I couldn't. He was good but the car wasn't. Once we went over a railway crossing and the car went into a real shimmy. He almost lost control. After that he drove very carefully and swore at it every time it seemed to have a mind of its own. Bill had been fruit picking before, and when he called in at the first orchard, he called them ranches, he was welcomed but told the crop had been destroyed by the blight. The farmer offered us use of the pickers' accommodation though, and as it was late and we had been driving all day, we were thankful for that. Next morning we set off again and stopped at another ranch Bill knew, and luckily work was available. Apples. Case after case of them we picked. There were other pickers there of course.

At the weekend we decided to go into town to get some more supplies, and on the way going down a steep hill, the car must have hit a pothole and went into a shimmy again. Bill lost control completely this time, and the car went off the road and rolled over. I was knocked out. When I came round, I managed to crawl out. The car was upside down. Then I noticed my hand was cut open and there was blood everywhere. I think the broken glass had done it. I tried to stop the bleeding with my other hand. Bill was no help. He'd hurt his leg and was limping around. Fortunately, another car load of pickers came along and stopped when they saw the accident. A woman jumped out and when she saw the state of my hand ran back to fetch a towel and insisted on binding my hand tightly. Then they crammed Bill and me into their car and drove to the doctor's in the town.

I was lucky to be examined by a doctor straight away. Whistling all the time he was. He took one look at my hand and said, 'That's a surgeon's job.' He promptly bandaged me up and said he would drive me to the hospital in Spokane. There, I was fixed up, stitched up, and then the doctor drove me all the way back to his own surgery. Some of the pickers had heard I'd got back and were waiting for me outside. I saw them through the window. I was worried about what would happen. I didn't have money to pay for the medical treatment and, of course, I was an illegal. I had no papers. Well, when the doctor went out of the room, I shot outside, joined the pickers, and told them to drive off quickly. I still feel bad about it because that doctor was very kind to me."

"But the stakes were very high for you," said Joan in a kindly voice. "You could have ended up in jail."

"I haven't got to that yet."

"Not really!" she exclaimed.

"Just wait," Richard paused, pleased to feel that now he had aroused her curiosity more than ever. "I got the bus back to Portland. My picking days were over with my hand being the way it was." With that he stretched his hand out for Joan to see the scars.

"It proves you haven't made it all up," she said. "So you went back to the Hindley's then?"

98

"Yes, I was still welcome there. Most of my hand healed up except for one small place on the palm. I couldn't work it out. I probed it with a toothpick and found the problem. A fragment of glass still in there. Once that was removed, it healed up quickly.

When I was fit for work again, I went down to the union office to see if there was anything going on the ships. The strike was over, and they said they would call me if anything turned up. A day or two later they did. There was a job for an ordinary seaman on a general cargo ship, the Masmara. So I took it. And what an eye opener that was. After British ships, the conditions were luxurious. Twice the pay. Watches four hours on and eight off. Clean bedding provided, and really good food. We sailed down the west coast to Los Angeles, and while we were in port there, I set up the block and tackle and bosun's chair to paint the funnel. I was used to using that sort of equipment and when the first mate saw that, he promoted me to seaman on full salary on the spot. Some of the crew had left the ship, and I think he didn't want to lose me.

Well, we left Los Angeles for New York via the Panama, and when we docked there it was getting close to Christmas. It was nice to go ashore again, but I didn't go far because I was worried about my lack of papers. Having a drink in a dockside bar was a treat, not that I drank much. A chap approached me there and asked me if I wanted a job. It turned out that the bar was full of a crew from a small tanker which was in dry dock for repairs. They all came from Fall River on Rhode Island, they said. It was about a hundred and fifty miles away and they were planning to go home to wives and families for Christmas. But they needed someone extra to help look after the ship while they were away."

"And you a complete stranger. They must have thought you looked honest."

"I think they were just desperate to get someone. When I said alright, they hailed a cab, took me down to the Masmara, where I signed off, got paid and grabbed my few belongings. Then they took me straight to Todd's dry dock and onto the tanker. It was the Irene W. Allen. Then they were off. Apart from me, there was just an engineer and one of the officers left on board. I said I'd do the cooking if they wanted. And you wouldn't believe the food they had in the cold store, - hams, turkeys, chickens, cuts of beef. Everything. We had a real feast on Christmas Day."

"You're making me feel hungry," said Joan, putting on the agony.

"It isn't me. It's this flaming cold. It must be ten degrees below out there. Has to be."

The parts of the inside of the ambulance where the metal body was exposed were dripping wet. It was their breath condensing. Only their body heat and the occasional heat from the stove stopped the interior from becoming an ice cave.

"New York's freezing in winter time. I've seen it on the newsreels," said Joan, returning the conversation to Richard's story.

"The crew came back in time for New Year's Eve celebrations. They took me with them down Fifth Avenue and to Radio City. The crowds were huge and everybody going mad. I enjoyed myself so much that I signed on as a crew member when the tanker was ready to go back to sea. It plied the Atlantic coast and the Gulf of Mexico. It was a comfortable life, but I ended up feeling an outsider. They'd all known each other for years and they were all married with families. I didn't have much in common with them, so I signed off in New York.

After a few weeks the weather was still cold, so I decided to take a bus south to Carolina. I knew it would be warmer there."

"Warm weather," said Joan, " it's hard to believe it exists."

"I'll light the stove. You brew up and I'll do my duty." He jumped out. "It's stopped snowing," he yelled out. For a few moments he gazed at the snowy wilderness, the valley and the *muelas*. "Now we'll soon be back in action, but we can't go anywhere 'til the road's cleared."

*   *   *

"Every time you go out you let the cold air in. Tell me, was it warmer in Carolina?"

"Oh yes, I knew it would be. The tanker used to put in at ports along the coast and it was always warm. Because of the Gulf Stream. That's a warm current that comes out of the Gulf of Mexico, runs up the east coast and then goes all the way across the Atlantic. It even affects Britain and Norway. It's why North Cape never freezes up."

"Thanks for the geography. I suppose you learnt those things at sea, or was it at that school? Anyway, what happened to you in Carolina? You hinted at having got into some sort of trouble."

Richard laughed. "Not in Carolina. When I got off the bus in Charleston, I booked in at the Seaman's Mission and went down to the union office to see if there was any work going. I did that every day while I was there and got quite friendly with the union chaps. Well, a Greek ship came in and the seamen on it claimed they had been underpaid. The union decided to board the vessel and the Board of Trade got involved as well. They used to inspect vessels to check if they were seaworthy or not. I was asked to join the boarding party because they knew I was a bosun and had been on lots of different ships. We found the ship in a terrible state, particularly from a safety point of view. Life boats that couldn't be released. Fire equipment jammed up. All that sort of thing. They impounded it and wouldn't let it leave port until it had been fixed up.

Just after that incident, an American tanker tied up and some of the crew came into the union office to report that the first mate and the bosun were quarrelling and had come to blows. It could only get worse, they said. The union reported it to the company and they were both fired. I think drink was the main cause of the problem. Cheap corn liquor that you could get for a dollar a pint, despite prohibition. The shipping company promoted the second mate to first mate, and the bosun to second mate. Then they were looking for a new bosun. I applied and got the job on the strength of my discharge letters from the Masmara and the Irene W. Allen. The new first mate wasn't too pleased that I got the job. He knew that I was aware of all that had been going on before and might start making trouble like the previous bosun. So I confronted him and told him that what had happened in the past was no concern of mine and I was there just to do my job. We got on alright after that apart from him not liking me telling him that the crew should be sober at all times. That was because when we left port for Galveston some of them were three sheets to the wind."

"That must have taken some courage seeing that you had just told him that all you wanted to do was your job."

"It was a safety issue and that's everyone's job".

Richard had done the right thing in the circumstances, she thought. He always does. But she kept her musings to herself. Instead, she just gave him an appraising look which he took as an invitation to continue.

"When we docked at Galveston, some of the crew went ashore. I didn't go with them. Because I was bosun, I preferred to keep my distance. After some time I went ashore by myself to look around and I hadn't got very far when a large black car stopped on the opposite side of the road. The two chaps in it looked official. Wearing suits and ties. The driver called me over. They were plain-clothes police and asked me who I was and what I was doing and so on. My accent must have been a give-away. They didn't believe I was an American. I'd said that I was because I was on an American ship. I couldn't have said much else. Well, the passenger got out, opened the back door and told me to get in and he jumped in beside me. I had to direct them to the tanker, and they took me on board and asked to see my cabin. The chap on watch must have must have wondered what was going on. When they looked through my clothing, the name tag in my suit was my real name, not Richard Daniel Buck. Moreover, the label said Made by Richard Howell, Tailors, Manchester, England. 'You're British ain't you?' one of them said. I had to admit it. They arrested me, took me down to the station with all my belongings, finger-printed me and put me in a cell. They spent a couple of days checking out whether I had a criminal record or not. I think my discharge letters from the Masmara and Irene W. Allen helped. They told me that I was to be deported as soon as a ship was available to take me to England."

He paused, as if expecting a negative reaction from Joan. But she said nothing. Just gave him a look of incredulity, but not disdain. There was even a hint of admiration, he thought. Surely she couldn't be admiring him for being deported. It forced him to say in a challenging tone, "So there you are. Now you know all about my murky past."

After what seemed like an eternity, she returned his enquiring gaze with a faraway look and said in a strangely detached voice, "I think we should get married."

Richard was stunned, speechless. His jaw dropped. It was a bolt from the blue. He had realised Joan was fond of him. She'd shown that more than once. First on the trip to Madrid. But he was unprepared for this. Joan was educated, middle class. He was working class, educated in the school of hard knocks. Had she really said that, he thought. The confirmation came not in words. She reached across and kissed him. Eventually he found his voice. "So being deported doesn't matter?"

"Not at all. Why should it?"

This time Richard kissed her. Even in his dreams, he had never believed it could come to this. "You mean when we get back to England? Getting married that is?"

"No, here! We will find someone from the British Battalion. The commissar will do the honours. He knows both of us and with you being in the Party, he's sure to agree."

Joan had decided.

7

TERUEL AGAIN

In the morning when Richard went to run the motor, he could hear the distant sound of gunfire and explosions from the direction of Teruel and then from the opposite direction a steady rumbling. It got louder. Joan had heard it too and jumped out to see the first signs of life for more than two days. They both knew the sound. Tanks. A small column of six tanks came into view. Russian tanks, each with just the head of one crew visible. Richard gave the clenched fist salute to the leading tanks, then with a sweep of his arm indicated that one of them should swing off the road to clear a path for the ambulance to get free. His gesture was understood and two of the tanks veered off the road towards the ambulance, cutting a wide trench through the snow. Only a little snow remained to be cleared manually to get the ambulance back on the road.

After the tanks was a long convoy of lorries and other military vehicles bringing supplies to the front. They waited until the last one had passed before they joined the convoy. Richard hung back some distance from the lorry in front of them.

"I wonder what we will find at the first aid post," said Joan.

But he was still going over in his mind what he had been telling her the previous night about his exploits in America. He had never told anyone before about his deportation for fear of what people would think of him. Now he wanted to finish the story even though they were about to plunge themselves back into the fray.

"I wasn't the only one deported back to Britain you know. There were two or three others. Every one of them had a tale to tell. One chap must have been in his sixties. His hair as white as this snow. What a life he'd had! Sent to Canada as a child migrant from Dr. Barnardo's Homes. Treated like a slave, he was. Escaped, that's what he said, escaped to the U.S. When he was older, he got mixed up in crime. Given twenty years in gaol when he was caught. When he was released, he lived the life of a hobo until he was accused of another serious crime which he said he never did and got another twenty years. And after all that, he was being deported back to the country that had got rid of him in the first place. I often think of that poor chap. What a life!"

Joan merely nodded to show she was listening as she stared out at the wintry landscape where only the steepest slopes of the *muelas* were free of snow. The low cloud afforded protection from aerial attack for the supply column and cast a menacing gloom over the scene. As they got nearer to Teruel it became clear that the fighting on the edge of the town was continuing. They were told that the Fascist garrison was close to surrender, but that Franco was still demanding that it fight on. Now that the Spanish army had the upper hand, casualties were fewer but still there were the frost bite cases.

On the eighth of January the Fascist garrison did surrender. Civilians were evacuated. No reprisals. They were Spanish. Victims of geography, trapped in the Fascist area. The victory had been achieved by the Spanish army. Indalecio Prieto had been in overall command but the surprise attack and encirclement had been achieved by Lister's Eleventh Division and Heredia's Eighteenth Army group. Along with the stoic defense of Madrid, it was the Republic's greatest military achievement. This time the International Brigades had been kept in reserve, training new recruits. The Fifteenth and the British Battalion were billeted at Alcorisa, one hundred miles to the northeast. After the fall of the town, Fred Copeman, the British commander, Sam Wild, his adjutant, and political commissar, Walter Tapsell, came down to see the situation for themselves. They had learnt that Richard and Joan were providing first aid services there and Tapsell sought them out when Copeman fell ill again. He had never fully recovered from wounds received on the Jarama Front. They picked him up straight away. He was a stretcher case and Joan went into the back of the ambulance with an English nurse, Mary, to attend to him. Wild and Tapsell rode in the front with Richard. The roads had been cleared of snow and the journey to Alcorisa went quickly. Copeman wanted Joan to stay with him. He had been told about her professional skills and dedication by Tapsell who had met her on the Aragón front the previous Autumn.

After they had transferred Copeman to a hospital bed, Joan asked Tapsell for a quiet word. He was surprised at being asked to perform a marriage ceremony, to say the least, but acquiesced given the firmness of Joan's request.

"You really marry each other," she said to him, as if to let Tapsell off the hook. "The minister is just the witness." So with no more ado, Joan went and got Richard, and they said their 'yes's' before the

Communist commissar in the hospital courtyard. No paperwork. Simply a vow to each other.

"Now you must kiss the bride," said Tapsell, with a wide grin. And after Richard had obeyed the order he added, "And now you'd better get back to the front, comrade, there is work to be done." After a second kiss, Joan went back to Copeman's bedside. He was still in pain. Something wrong is going on inside there, she thought, looking at his pallor and clenched mouth. He was a surgical case if ever there was one. But what was it?

*   *   *

When Richard got back to Teruel, he found most roads were cleared of snow. He was sent to a different first aid post where he was given control of three other ambulances. He was pleased with the set-up. Two of the other drivers were Brigaders like himself and one was Spanish. All four ambulances had Spanish first aiders to look after the wounded, and in addition there was a number of *camilleros*, stretcher-bearers, to assist in loading. As the Fascist counter-attack was gathering strength, helped by clearer skies, there was a steady flow of casualties coming in. The practice was to fill up each ambulance in turn before dispatching it, unless someone was so critical that he had to be evacuated immediately. They were taking them to a hospital set up in a large cave a few miles back from the first aid post. The staff there were all Spanish.

Things were working well as far as Richard was concerned, until one of the ambulances driven by a fair-haired Brigader didn't return from a trip. Perhaps he's been given another assignment, he thought. He decided to take the next trip in just to check it out. After he and his Spanish first aider had dropped off their casualties, they made their enquiries about the missing ambulance. A Spanish officer at the hospital, a commissar, verified that the ambulance had brought wounded in. He was quite certain, given the description of the driver as being the fair-haired one. He had seen him many times before and assumed he had gone back to the first aid post. The officer could see by Richard's reaction that he was angry. It looked as if the Brigader had absconded. Now he was down to three ambulances, and the fighting was getting heavier as the Fascists brought in more fresh troops.

Desertions were taking place. Richard had heard that those caught were being shot by firing squads drawn from the deserters' own battalions. Fred Copeman wouldn't have had any of that, he thought. He believed Copeman's view was that volunteers should not be shot. They were neither professional nor conscripted soldiers. He had heard him say that. Nevertheless, it was a dilemma. Desertions damaged morale, particularly if it was believed that they were getting clean away. Announcing that they had been shot while trying to desert, or putting them in front of a firing squad of their own comrades, might convince those in the front line that they were better off where they were if their minds turned to escaping the shells, bombs and bullets.

Self-inflicted wounds were another problem at this time. Comrades were coming in from the front with shattered hands. Mostly right hands. They were usually in great pain and had to be taken to the hospital. Richard wondered what happened to them as they would no longer be able to fire rifles. With the help of his Spanish first aider and appropriate gestures, he was able to put that question to the hospital commissar.

"Come with me," he beckoned, and led the way up a side road to where there was a long earth-covered shed. From it there were constant cries of pain, wailing and calls for help.

"What will become of them?" asked Richard through his first aider. The officer didn't reply in words. Perhaps he didn't want to say. He just shrugged his shoulders. Richard suspected the worst. They'll be shot, he thought, but who will decide? He saw self-inflicted wounds as defeatism. Although he was a non-combatant, he was very committed to the cause and was certain the Fascists would be defeated in the end. Good would prevail over evil, he believed, but that wouldn't happen if comrades used self-mutilation as a way out.

On the way back to the first aid post, the ambulance suddenly cut out. He was fearful of being immobilised in such circumstances. You were just a sitting duck if a German or Italian pilot took a liking to you. Fortunately, he thought he knew what the problem might be and that if he was right, he would be able to fix it quickly. He was right. The main lead from the distributor to the coil had broken free and cut off the spark; all due to the jolting on the rough roads. He was able to wedge it back in with a matchstick as a temporary repair, and with a feeling of much relief, got underway again. But that sense of relief didn't last long. He saw an explosion lift up the road like a miniature volcanic eruption a quarter of a mile ahead. He swerved the ambulance off the road and dived for the protection of a culvert. It was already occupied. Two soldiers had sought cover there before him. They were sitting calmly smoking as if they hadn't a trouble in the world. Richard grinned at them. They recognised his cap badge and nodded back. One pointed his forefinger upwards saying, "*Fascista, Fascista.*" So it was an aircraft, thought Richard. A bomb not a shell.

The action taking place was largely confined to the daytime. The Fascists were pushing at the Republican lines in their attempt to win back Teruel.. With only three ambulances, dealing with the wounded from the front was an increasingly difficult job. Joan was still away looking after Copeman. He missed her. He hoped she was safe. Nowhere was really safe with enemy aircraft bombing behind the lines, targeting supply depots and transport lines. And he was still angry about the loss of the fourth ambulance.

Still in this anxious state of mind, he sent two full ambulances together back to the hospital, one driven by a Brigader, the other by the Spanish driver. After some time, the Spanish driver returned, explaining that he had been delayed by having to fill up on petrol. However, the Brigade driver was a long time turning up and Richard started wondering if he too had absconded. Eventually he did arrive, just as the post came under air attack. At first the *camilleros*, at the post had thought the aircraft friendly. "*Nuestros*," they called out. But they weren't 'ours' and when the bombs started falling, the cry went up, "*Fascistas*". The brigade driver arrived just as that was happening. However, instead of leaving the vehicle and diving for cover, he started to manoeuvre it as if to drive off in the direction he had come from. It wasn't possible to make a U-turn because of lack of space, so he had to reverse. Convinced that he was about to leave the post, Richard, who had by this time grabbed his automatic, leapt onto the running board shouting, "*Alto, alto*," while thrusting his pistol through the open window of the cab. He was on the passenger side and the Spanish first aider in the cab, probably fearing for his life, tried to push him off. But he was not to be easily dislodged as his own first aider came up behind pushing him forwards to stop him from falling back.

The explosion in Richard's hand took him by surprise. The bullet grazed the chest of the first aider and went upwards through the jaw of the driver. Death was instant. With all the pushing and shoving, Richard could hardly believe what had happened. He had killed a fellow Brigader. But his anguish was diminished because he felt he'd saved the ambulance. He went round to the other side of the cab and pulled out the dead Brigader and with the help of a *camillero* put him in the back of his own ambulance. As he did this he realised why he had been late returning. He smelt of wine. That the Brigader had been drunk now added to Richard's torment. Had he been sober he would have acted differently, but then drinking on the job is no excuse. Guilt and justification were fighting a battle in Richard's mind. Justification was winning. The security of an ambulance was a priority with comrades being wounded at an increasing rate. The Spanish first aider with the grazed chest jumped out. He knew that it was only a graze. He had been lucky but was worried that he might be implicated in the Brigader's action. An accomplice. However, Richard ignored him. He called on the Spanish driver to take over the ambulance and drive to the hospital with the body of the Brigader and explain what had happened.

By this time the bombing had ceased. One good thing about bombing is that it doesn't last long, thought Richard. They come over, drop them and leave. Five minutes of fear and hell. After a while he drove to the hospital himself, leaving the other ambulance at the post. Within a mile he was forced to stop. The road had been cratered, and a group of soldiers and locals were busy filling it in. He jumped out and joined in. The exercise made him feel better. Labouring with his Spanish comrades helped to remind him why he was there, why he was in Spain. By the time he got to the hospital, he was feeling much better with himself. The commissar already knew what had happened. He conveyed his acceptance of it all with a shrug, as if to say, these things happen in war. He knew that Richard was committed to protecting the ambulances. And, that he was a member of the Party.

*   *   *

Not long after this incident the Spanish driver and his ambulance were sent to a different post, and a day or so later, Richard was directed to work on another sector. Fascist forces were building up to the northwest of Teruel. The loss of the city had dented Franco's pride and he was determined to recover it. On the seventeenth of January there was a temporary breakthrough of Republican defences. On the nineteenth the International Brigades were brought in, including the Fifteenth and the British Battalion, now under the acting command of Bill Alexander. Headquarters were established close to the city centre. Joan returned to the front, replacing Richard's Spanish first aider. They were re-deployed in support of the Fifteenth Brigade and established a post on a hill close to the front. Wounded were ferried to a hospital in a stone building further back.

They were both glad to be back together and working as a team again. The workload varied with the level of action. At times they went into the centre of Teruel to pick up petrol and other supplies. It was always risky as the Fascists now occupied some of the *muelas* and their snipers were active. On these occasions Joan would join him in the cab, partly for company, but also because another pair of eyes was a valuable safety precaution. If there were wounded needing attention, that was a different matter. On one occasion driving through the shattered town, Richard spotted a lone figure picking his way along a rubble-strewn street. He was only about fifty yards away.

"It's a Brigader," said Joan, "with that beret and rucksack it has got to be. Let's see who it is."

"I don't believe this," muttered Richard, as they drew closer, "but I'm sure it's Dr. Bradsworth from the Battalion. I had a lot to do with him at Jarama and he came to Huete at least once."

As they came alongside, the Brigader paid no attention expecting the vehicle to pass him. His slight figure bent under the weight of his rucksack and his dejected expression spoke of weariness.

"Dr. Bradsworth." The shout startled him. Then raising an arm towards the ambulance, he gave a broad smile of recognition.

"I've seen you around," he said.

"Do you want a lift or anything?"

"Have you any tea or sugar?" he asked.

Joan reached across. "Get in and we'll pull over by the cathedral. It's safer there."

After stopping, Joan introduced herself and invited Bradsworth to come into the back and have a hot drink. They hadn't had a break all morning. Richard pumped up the primus, and soon they were enjoying hot mugs of tea and listening to Bradsworth's tale of woe.

"Yesterday I was walking in the town and my Spanish assistant kept walking a few paces behind me. I found this annoying. I knew he was doing this in deference to me, you know, the doctor bit. I stopped and said in the best Spanish I could muster, 'We are comrades. That means you walk with me, not behind me.' He understood, and was pleased to walk alongside, as if it was a promotion. Barely a minute later, a sniper's bullet shot him dead and ripped through my rucksack. The bullet punctured my tin of condensed milk which oozed all over my tea and sugar and other bits and pieces. Well I was able to clean some things up, but the tea and sugar were beyond salvation."

Bradsworth looked forlorn again, despite the tea and the company.

"If I hadn't insisted on him walking alongside, I would have copped it."

"I suppose he got what many at the front hope for, if you're going to cop it, let it be quick," said Richard, trying to find something positive to say.

"And he was in a good frame of mind," added Joan, "after his promotion, that is."

Bradsworth gave a wan smile, as if to say, I suppose that's something. He collected the tea and sugar Joan had packed for him, and after brief farewells and take-cares, jumped out into the plaza and disappeared up one of the many narrow *calles* around the cathedral.

*　　　*　　　*

The ferrying of wounded from first-aid posts to the hospital was constant. There was always the satisfaction of getting comrades to treatment in time, and also the obvious appreciation of comrades for the attention they received when they came in or while they were in transit. But there were few diversions or much in the way of light relief, although they did have each other's company and the night time refuge of the ambulance.

When they had bunked down for the night, Joan still sought escape from the day's tribulations in Richard's stories.

"You have yet to tell me what happened to you after you arrived back in England, after you had been deported from America. And how did you become a driver?"

"I went to my Aunt Ethel's in Marsden."

"Why didn't you go to your mother's?"

"She'd remarried, as I told you, and her husband had left the job in Catterick and they had moved to London. Anyway, I suppose I wanted to get back to where I felt I belonged."

"I'm surprised you felt you belonged anywhere by that time. Did you find work there?"

"There wasn't much around. The Labour Exchange told me about a whaling ship, the Southern Cross, which operated out of South Georgia, needing crew. I took a look at it. It was anchored in the Tyne waiting for orders. I wasn't so sure about going to sea again and rather than just sit around waiting, I decided to learn to drive with the British School of Motoring in Newcastle. It was my good luck that the instructor lived in South Shields and in addition to lessons around South Shields for which I was paying, if he had to go into Newcastle, he'd ask me to drive him in and out. All for nothing. He liked to have the company, I suppose."

Joan laughed. "You were paying him with stories, were you?"

116

"Well I don't know about that. We just got on. And that's how I came to get my driving licence. Fortunately, I had the money to pay for the lessons from what I had saved up at sea. My allotments from my pay used to go into my bank account in South Shields."

"Sounds like you became a petty capitalist," she teased.

"You're joking. But I did buy a car after I got my licence. An open tourer with a canvas top. Second hand, of course."

"There you are. With all that unemployment and poverty on Tyneside, people probably thought you were a toff when they saw you driving round."

"Perhaps some did, but I was unemployed myself. Fortunately a special government unemployment programme had been set up, and people could apply to get on a number of six month long courses in a variety of trades. Because I could drive, I got on a motor mechanics' course at Wallsend. I still got paid the dole while I was on it..Fourteen shillings a week. They kept you at it, eight till five, stripping and reassembling engines, gearboxes and differentials."

"So that's how you came to be a mechanic, as well as a driver." It was more of a statement than a query.

"You haven't heard it all yet. After getting my certificate from that course, I saw adverts in the papers for a chauffeur and motor maintenance course at a Rolls Royce school near London. With my mother now living there, I was keen to get on the course and stay with her. I was accepted, paid my ten pound fee, and better still, was made really welcome by my step-father."

"It wasn't your stories again was it?"

Now it was his turn to laugh. He went on. "The Rolls course was thorough like the other, but the main thing was the driving. Changing gear without jolting was a skill that had to be practised, particularly changing down, when you had to double-declutch. The maintenance part involved greasing, changing the oil and balancing the wheels. You had to adjust the spokes to do that."

"Did you get a certificate for that as well?"

"No. There was a Rolls Royce certificate which was a good qualification, but you had to drive and look after the same car for two years and then take their test to get it. And I never did that."

Joan was wondering what all this training led to. "So what did you do?"

"A barrister wanted a chauffeur to drive him in his Bentley to and from his chambers at Rotten Row. They are not much different from Rolls Royces to drive. I got the job and they had me kitted out with a uniform and peak cap."

Joan laughed, "I can remember hearing about that back at Huete. Everyone found it hard to believe."

He was pleased she found it so funny. "Anyway, I didn't like the master servant relationship, and when my cousin Bill told me about a job going for a driver with a chemical company in Welwyn Garden City, I went to check it out. The factory was closed when I got there, but the owners were on the premises. They lived next to it. They were a married couple, the Earnshaws. We had a long talk about the job and what I'd done before. Well they offered me it there and then, so I accepted. The barrister wasn't at all happy about me leaving, but he couldn't do anything about it."

"I remember you talking about the Earnshaws in the garage back at Huete. You said that he used to let you have the car for the week-end if it was spare, and that his wife would bring the workers mugs of tea or cocoa at break-times."

"You've got a good memory. They were good people. When this war broke out, they were as outraged as the rest of us at Franco's attempt to overthrow the elected government. I can remember Mr. Earnshaw thundering, 'if it is elected by all the people, it has the right to rule so long as it abides by the constitution.' He put a lot of emphasis on the words 'all' and 'constitution'. What exactly is the constitution, Joan?"

"That is a hard one. It's the rules that govern the Government. I think that's the best way of putting it."

"We talked about not much else but the Spanish situation at breaks, and when there was a call for volunteers, we talked about that too. Many of the fellows were married and had families and didn't think it was right for them to volunteer. And you know the rest. Inquiring at Communist Party Headquarters in King Street. Being sent to Spanish Medical Aid when they realised I could drive. And coming out here with those four ambulances. Then I met you," he said with an air of finality

"Not quite! A lot happened before you met me. I found that out on the road to Madrid."

*   *   *

Fascist attacks on the Republican defences around Teruel increased in intensity at the time the International Brigades were brought in. Accurate artillery and trench mortar fire and the strafing and bombing of Republican positions from the air by Italian Fiats became their daily bread. The weather was still bitterly cold; the landscape still snow covered. The ambulances worked from dawn till dusk as Fascist breakthroughs were followed by Republican counter-attacks.

The Fifteenth Brigade was pulled out for rest on the third of February after two weeks of heavy action. Richard and Joan had the ambulance on stand-by, looking out for comrades who needed treatment as the battalions filed back through the streets of Teruel. They looked as if they hadn't had a change of clothing all the time they had been at the front. The Americans had solved this problem by raiding an abandoned clothing store and helping themselves to all manner of attire; formal suits, tights, sombreros, gaudy waist-coats, anything that half-fitted. Whooping and yelling, they dragged or carried their military equipment in a bizarre fancy dress parade. This was no retreat or defeat was the message of their antics, just a rotation of units. The British conveyed their message in a different way, marching in formation through the streets of the town. Shouts of 'hermanos' greeted them.

Richard slowly patrolled the lines of marchers, Joan looking for any who needed treatment. They identified some, but they were reluctant to fall out, reluctant to leave their comrades. Later it was decided to take a few of the worst cases to a hospital at Valdeganga de Cuenca. There, they were surprised to find Nan Green in charge, and they were all delighted to see each other again. Joan had a long chat with Nan. They seem to have a lot in common thought Richard. Energetic, good organisers and both Londoners. Out of the conversation rose the idea of going over to Huete to see what was happening there.

However, when Nan pulled out photographs of her two young children, and started telling Joan about how different they were, Richard decided to opt out and go for a brisk walk round and about the hospital. When he returned he found them engaged in a much more earnest conversation. Nan cut it short as soon as she saw him, causing him to wonder what it was all about. Joan salvaged the ensuing silence with, "We'd better be off." They all embraced. Nan looked forlorn at the parting despite Joan's attempt at a reassuring smile. "Now for Huete," said Richard, trying to ease his discomfort.

* * *

The drive relaxed them. They were well away from the front and the sounds of explosions. There was snow about, particularly on the Altos de Cabrejas but the roads were reasonably clear.

"What was all that about then. Why did Nan clam up when I came back?"

"Well, she knows you're in the Party and she is being given a bad time by a Party fanatic at the hospital. She feels she doesn't know who to trust and is thinking of resigning."

"Surely it can't be that bad."

"It is, because that fanatic happens to be her boss. The Chief Medical Officer. He's German. A Doctor Kretzschmar. Apparently once imprisoned by the Nazis, an experience he parades as a badge of honour. He made advances toward her despite knowing she was married and a mother, but she spurned him. Put him in his place. What really made matters worse between them was that Nan went on to have an fling with a patient. British he was. Recovering from his wounds. Kretzschmar, out of jealousy and anger started challenging her commitment to the cause. She thinks he has denounced her as a political risk to the authorities in Albacete."

"They won't believe that. She was in the Party long before she came to Spain. A true believer."

"I hope you're right, but they may think she has become disillusioned. Others have. Disaffected they call it."

Nan, disaffected. Richard couldn't accept that. After all, she had left her children with grandparents to come to Spain. That's commitment. Joan was thinking much the same.

When they arrived at Huete they found some Brigaders still convalescing. They seemed to be doing well but were not yet fit enough to return to the front. The bad news was that Thomas Kerr, the *tendencia*, had died. Consumption, T.B., they were told. Both had enjoyed Thomas's company and Irish wit and his help with fitting out the ambulance. The hospital was almost empty compared with how it had been. Seeing there was plenty of room, they decided to bed down there for the night, talking with the staff and Brigaders they knew long into it.

Next morning they set off after breakfast to return to Valdeganga. It was again a pleasant drive with no wounded to worry about. Coming into the town of Cuenca where Richard hoped to pick up petrol at an outlet he had been to several times before, they found another ambulance filling up there. He immediately recognised the driver as an American comrade he had known from the Jarama front. In the short cordial reunion, he introduced Joan and they exchanged what news they had. The American's news was bad news. There had been a major Fascist breakthrough on the Teruel front. They had attacked from the west, well north of the city, towards Alfambra and Perales. If the offensive continued, the Spanish army could be trapped in Teruel, just as the Fascist garrison was in December.

"I need to get back," he said, and added with a grim expression, "there'll be plenty to do." And he sped off.

*   *   *

When they got back to Valdeganga, Bill Alexander, acting commander of the British Battalion, Sam Wild, second-in-command and George Fletcher were there. They needed transport to Brigade headquarters which was now well north of the city of Teruel. It was getting late, and it was obvious that if they set off there and then, they would be travelling much of the way in darkness. So the journey was postponed until the next day. The drive to Teruel was uneventful. Aircraft were seen from time to time but they had other targets and had no reason to suspect that an ambulance was carrying the commanders of the British Battalion. As they got close to the front, Alexander told Richard to pull over. They all got out stretching and exercising to stimulate circulation while simultaneously stamping feet numbed from the bitter cold. There was a valley carved into the Meseta to the left of the vehicle and snow covered sierras framed the scene. All surveyed it with a sense of trepidation, having heard of the breakthrough. The dull thud of shells exploding in the distance was the only sound. There were no aircraft around. Alexander broke the spell, disrupting the private thoughts of each of them, with his characteristic stuttering. "If the F-Fascists are over there, it's not t-too bad, but if they are over here, it's b-bloody awful." He went on to explain his concerns mainly to Wild as they clambered back into the ambulance. Eventually, they reached the place where Alexander and the others wanted to be dropped off. It must have been the new location of the Fifteenth Brigade headquarters, but there wasn't really much there. As they left the ambulance Alexander voiced concern that the Brigades were going to be pushed back into the fray after only a few days of rest. But he had to accept it. They were now part of the Spanish army.

Richard drove on from there to a position close to Alfambra. There were many vehicles in the area including lorries, tanks and other ambulances. Joan asked him to stop so that she could check out the medical situation with a view to finding an existing first aid post or even establishing one. When she got back, she directed him to a position which was protected from bombing by a high cliff. It was a safe place, at least for the time being. With there being lots of vehicles around, some damaged beyond repair, it occurred to Richard that there was the possibility of being able to salvage spare parts. After scouting around, he gave the Wales as thorough a service as he could. However, they didn't stay in that protected position for long. A tactical retreat was the order of the day. He never thought of any of the movements of position as retreats. He thought of them as merely movements from one sector to another. His was a naive belief that because the cause was just it would succeed. Serious losses were merely temporary setbacks.

The tanks moved out first, then the heavy transport towing artillery, followed by the medical team. Later in the day, they found the British Battalion drawn up on the side of the road. Some field showers were being set as the men hadn't had a shower since their re-engagement in action on the 9th. February. Joan, who was now well known in the Battalion, took the opportunity to check out the fitness of the men as they passed through the showers. It was a quick and efficient way of checking to see if they had unreported injuries or minor wounds that needed treating. It reminded Richard of going through the showers back at the Gateshead school.

Later that day a Battalion meeting was held. Sam Wild was now acting Battalion commander and George Fletcher second-in-command, as Alexander had been wounded in the shoulder. Political commissar Tapsell was also there. Details of the last action were being discussed. Wild said that confusion had occurred in the heat of battle because an order to move to the north had been misunderstood and one company had moved to the south. "A complete balls-up!" he said, and suddenly realising Joan was there, he apologised for his coarse language. Chivalry even in a time of crisis.

The Fifteenth Brigade was on the move and was next involved in action at Segura de los Baños well to the north. The plan was to advance west to cut Fascist supply lines with a view to reducing pressure on Teruel. However, only a few hill tops were taken. It was too little too late. The Spanish commander, Campesino, abandoned Teruel narrowly escaping the encircling Fascists. And even then, thousands of Republican comrades were captured along with large quantities of equipment. The achievements of December and January were lost in February.

*   *   *

Towards the end of the month, Richard was ordered to take the Battalion commanders to see Copeman in hospital at Alcañiz. Wild, Fletcher, Tapsell and a Spanish *tendencia* were in the group and, of course, Joan. The commanders reported to Copeman on a regular basis as he had never relinquished his position and sought to remain in ultimate command even from his hospital bed. This was never resented by his senior colleagues. They held him in high regard. They all trooped into the small ward and, with the exception of Richard, they all sat around Copeman's bed. Richard thought military matters were no concern of his, and they weren't. But Joan took part as did the *tendencia*. Plans for dealing with the medical needs of the Battalion were every bit as important as supplies. Both could be the difference between life and death, victory and defeat.

Richard's attention had been caught by another bed in the ward and as it was empty and the others were all engrossed in discussion, he decided not to break in and ask if it was alright for him to have a rest. He just lay down and in no time he was out like a light. Catching a nap without risking the safety of yourself and your comrades is a rare luxury in war. When he woke up, there were no reprimands. His exhaustion was understood. He was, however, questioned about the loss of ambulances at Teruel, and about the incident in which he had used force to save one. But again there were no reprimands.

It was late when they all set off to return to the Battalion, and as darkness fell, a thick fog formed. The commanders were all in the back of the ambulance unaware of the increasing difficulty Joan and Richard were having in working out where they were.

"This is as bad as a London fog," she exclaimed, finding her role of navigator almost impossible.

"You should know," was the sparse reply.

As she peered through the windscreen a sense of fear suddenly gripped her.

"Richard," she whispered, "I think we're behind enemy lines, and we have the entire command of the British Battalion with us. Those figures over there with the leather leggings," she said, peering through the fog, "they look like Fascist officers. They are too smart for our lot."

"What the hell!" he muttered, wondering what he should do.

"Turn around gently so as not to arouse attention," she advised.

"Gently does it." Talking to himself under his breath, he manoeuvred the vehicle as inconspicuously as he himself wanted to be at that moment. Thank God I'm not wearing my beret, he thought. That could have really alerted them if they were to see it.

They both breathed out simultaneously as the ambulance moved out of danger. Somehow they found their way back to the Battalion but they never told their charges that they had come within a whisker of being captured. That night as they settled down in the ambulance, Richard said, "We were lucky those in the back didn't make a commotion when we stopped and turned around."

"I was just thinking the same. I suspect they may have been half asleep." And it wasn't long before they were asleep themselves.

8

ARAGON

If February was a bad month, March was worse. The International Brigades were transferred north to the Aragón front. The main Brigade base was at Caspe. Before they had left the Alfambra area, Joan had managed to restock the ambulance with blankets and medical supplies. In addition, food supplies and coffee, tea, sugar and water were obtained. It gave her a sense of being in control to be as ready as possible for any emergency.

In the first week of March they established their first aid post in the *pueblo* of Lécera, close to part of the front manned by the Fifteenth Brigade. A small wooden hut provided a base. *Camilleros* were allocated to the position and extra canvas stretchers, blankets and water were stored in the hut. A field hospital had been set four miles further back. Towards the end of the week, Richard and Joan were called to Brigade headquarters to be told by the American commander, Robert Merriman, that a major Fascist offensive was imminent and that all women in the area were to be evacuated.

Merriman had recently been promoted to Chief of Staff of the Brigade. Richard had known him from the Jarama Front. He was a tall striking figure with a direct manner and always showed concern for his men.Now it looked as if he was saying that Joan herself had to be evacuated.

"Do you think that Merriman's order included you?" Richard asked as they drove back to the first aid post. Adopting the clipped tone of a hospital matron, Joan replied, "In situations like this, it is better that one does not seek clarification. One might get an answer that one might not want."

What's all this bloody one stuff, thought Richard, why can't you just say you? But all he said was, "O.K." It was an expression he'd got from the Americans. He had got so used to Joan being with him that the thought of going back to working the ambulance without her was unthinkable.

"The real issue is," asserted Joan, "we are a good team and we are needed."

Merriman's warning of a major offensive was an understatement. It proved to be a massive attack as three Fascist army groups swept westwards towards Belchite, Caspe and Alcañiz, backed by squadrons of Messerschmitts, Heinkels, Dorniers and Junkers of the German Condor Legion and the Fiats, Savoias and Romeos of the Italian forces. They were also supported by two hundred light tanks and superior artillery.

Not long after arriving back at the post, all hell was let loose. First came the bombs and then the shelling. One shell took the steeple off the church. A Fascist shell at that! Neither of them had experienced anything like it before. They were in the front line not the usual mile behind it. A retreat was underway and large numbers of soldiers were coming through, not just the wounded.

An American officer, seeing the ambulance outside the hut, yelled out from his staff car, "You've got to move out right now, buddy, or you'll be ketchup."

"Half my supplies are in the hut. I can't just abandon them," Richard shouted back above the din.

Joan, who was treating an injured comrade in the back of the ambulance, had heard the frantic conversation, and made for the hut to start bringing in the equipment.

"Leave it to me. You go with the American," insisted Richard.

Hesitating only for a moment, she dashed over to the car. The American called out, "There's a white stone building standing on its own about six miles east of here, you can set up your next post there. The nurse will be waiting for you."

The nurse, thought Richard, that nurse is my wife, but she was already in the car and moving out. With the help of the *camilleros*, he frantically transferred supplies from the hut to the ambulance. They wanted to come with him, but he insisted that the ambulance was reserved for the wounded only. They understood. They had to join the rest fleeing on foot.

As he left the post, he decided to avoid the main road going to the east as it was being shelled, and at any time German or Italian aircraft could come over to bomb and strafe. He took to the minor tracks north of the main road in the belief that if he roughly parallelled it, he was bound to come to the white building. The landscape was barren and open, and he felt exposed. He tried to reassure himself with the thought that at least he was not an artillery target. He picked out a particular peak on the horizon to guide his navigation, as the tracks twisted this way and that, and the forks and junctions tested his spatial sense.

Suddenly, in an otherwise empty landscape, he was surprised to see a distant, solitary figure right in his chosen path. He took his automatic out from under the seat and placed it on his lap where he could easily grab it. It's not likely to be a Fascist, he thought, but you can't be too careful. As he drew nearer, he could see that the person seemed to be surveying the landscape in his direction. There was a frantic wave. It was Joan.

"I saw you long before you saw me," she cried out, as he jumped out of the cab. "I thought at times you were going to miss me. You would be coming my way and then you would turn off and look as if you were going to miss me by a mile."

"Well I didn't and that's all that matters." There was tension in his voice. He kissed her, gave her a great big bear hug and kissed her again, undeterred by the distant explosions.

"I'm not sure whether I preferred the comradely hug or the marital kiss," she teased, as they got into the ambulance. When they set off, they decided to head back to the main road to check whether the mobile hospital was still in operation. At the point where they reached the road, they seemed to be out of the range of the Fascist artillery. They soon found the hospital, but it was in the process of being taken down. The patients had already been evacuated further east. There was nothing for them to do, so they turned back off the main road in search of the white stone building. It's isolation from other buildings made it easy to find. When they reached it, they were surprised to find the main door open. They went in and were confronted by the most unwarlike sight. There, sitting in front of an open fire was the American, with legs outstretched, warming himself. He looked utterly relaxed and totally removed from the drama of the day.

"Make yourselves at home," he said, with a sweep of his hand in the direction of other chairs. They accepted the invitation and talked about the morning's events and what to expect next. They just didn't know, so Joan resolved to keep their supplies in the ambulance. They just could not rely on any position becoming even half permanent.

The situation was far from comfortable however, despite the warm fire. The sounds of action were everywhere even though they were some distance away. Their conversation was soon interrupted by a man in railway uniform. He said he was from the nearby station. He had seen the ambulance arriving and had come over to tell them that there were people sheltering at the station and that many of them were wounded.

"We'd better check things out," said Richard. They moved outside to the ambulance and Joan told the railwayman to climb in beside her to show them the way. When the station came into view, the railway man pointed out the building. Richard stopped the ambulance outside what looked like a hall. The railwayman jumped out. Richard turned the ambulance around so that the back faced the hall to make it easier to receive any stretcher cases and, if necessary, to be able to make a quick getaway. He always did that. Joan understood his reasons for the manoeuvre. She always valued his sense of danger and foresight. He's better than an insurance policy, she thought. Then just as he switched off the motor, they heard the railwayman yell out, "*Ambulancia, ambulancia,*" as he opened the large doors to the hall. At that, people surged forward hoping for treatment or evacuation or both. Most were gripped with fear at the constant sounds of battle.

"Bloody hell!" exploded Richard. "We've got a right problem here." Joan passed him his rifle. They both jumped out. There must have been twenty of them pressing towards the back of the ambulance. Joan rose to the occasion putting on her most authoritative voice in the best Spanish she could muster. Her tone always worked with the Brigaders and she hoped it would work with these poor Spanish civilians. She held up her hand to gain their attention. "*Sólo para los heridos*. Only for the wounded," she told them bluntly. "*Sólo para los heridos*," she repeated. The crowd fell back, perhaps realising that one ambulance could not evacuate them all. She moved through them looking for any who were in serious need of treatment. The two she selected were still back in the hall in no fit condition to join in the rush. She went back to the ambulance for stretchers, enlisted the assistance of four able-bodied men from those outside the hall and with their help, managed to get them on to the stretchers and into the back of the ambulance. She asked the railwayman to reassure those being left behind that further help would be coming. Of course she was in no position to guarantee that. It will give them some hope, she rationalised. She got into the back with the wounded, both to start examining them and also to make sure that the others did not try to get in. Richard waited for the back door to slam and drove back to the white building. After treating their wounds, which had been caused by shrapnel, she left both of them on stretchers in the warmth of the house. That in itself was a great comfort after the coldness of the hall. At this stage neither of them had any idea of where they could take the wounded for further treatment as the Republican lines were being broken and the position of medical support teams close to the front was changing all the time.

Casualties started arriving at the white house. Mostly Americans. Joan had to improvise quickly. She used the ambulance for treatment and the house as a ward. At dusk there was a lull in the action and no more casualties were being brought in. They were both concerned about the fate of the Brigade and the British Battalion after the Fascist breakthrough. Darkness fell early so they decided to find out what had happened. They drove back to the main road and turned west towards the front. They thought that would give them the best chance of finding the Brigade.

They drove slowly down the road passing the site where the mobile hospital had been. Some distance further on some figures stepped out directly in front of them. They had to stop. It was the Brigade. The tall commanding figure of Merriman came forward and asked if they had any water. Joan gave him two full leather bottles and asked him where the British Battalion was. Further down the road, was the reply. So they moved on and soon came across another group of men. It was the Battalion. George Fletcher came up, then Sam Wild and the *tendencia*. Sam was shivering and Richard offered him his sheepskin jacket which he gladly accepted. Joan invited them into the back of the ambulance and gave the three of them a nip of brandy.

"Unfortunately, I haven't enough for all the boys," she said.

Richard and Joan were told that the previous headquarters had been overrun by the Fascists. That was a blow for them. When they were with the Brigade at Alfambra, they had left a few personal items in the keeping of headquarters, with a view to carrying only what was essential in the ambulance.

"Well, it looks like we have lost a few of our things," said Joan, "but others have lost a whole lot more than that."

"I'm glad you're philosophical about it ," responded Sam. "You had better get back to the first aid post. There'll be plenty of work for you tomorrow. And thanks for the jacket." That said , they all got out of the back and bade their farewells. Richard turned the ambulance around, and they slowly retraced their route back to the white house through the dark.

*   *   *

The next day, the balloon went up again. The bombing and shelling were ferocious.There were further Fascist breakthroughs and Republican forces had in places retreated in panic, sometimes throwing away their rifles and ammunition to make a more speedy escape. They had good cause to fear capture by the Fascists. Having heard about the massacres of prisoners at Málaga and Badajoz, they knew not to expect mercy from Mussolini's Italians or Franco's Moors.

After one of their trips to pick up the wounded, Joan and Richard arrived back at the first aid post to find there about a dozen men who had become separated from the British Battalion. Despite their distress, their main concern was to get back to the Battalion.

"Right lads," Richard said, "It will be safer if we wait until it's nearly dark. There'll not be much action then and it will be easier to find it."

So they lay around the house resting, and Joan managed to rustle up some food and drink for them. When the firing became more sporadic, Richard decided that it would be a good time to go as they would be able to see their way better than when it became fully dark."

"Alright lads, into the back of the ambulance," he shouted. They all roused themselves, and piled in. Joan helped cram them in, but the last one, holding his light machine gun, wouldn't fit.

"You can't leave me behind," he protested.

"You can come in the front," said Joan, "we'll be cramped up but we'll manage." And so they set off with Joan squeezed between Richard and a machine gun and gunner.

He drove slowly with a great sense of trepidation. He made for the same main road where they had found the Battalion the day before. When they reached it, a major retreat was in progress. Tanks were moving away from the front with their gun barrels swivelled back to face it, so that they could return any enemy fire. Also there were lorries pulling artillery pieces.

"At least the equipment is being saved," commented Joan, mindful of the huge loss of materials at Teruel.

Richard didn't answer. He was concentrating on weaving his way in second gear through the retreating traffic, ever alert for any vehicle turning into his path presuming nothing would be going the other way.

"There's something going on up ahead." The machine gunner was the first to see it. "Rifle fire and some explosions," he added.

No sooner had he said that than someone leapt seemingly from nowhere onto the running board of the ambulance. Shouting, "*Alto, alto!*" in a thick Slavic rather than Spanish accent, the assailant thrust a pistol in Richard's face. His reaction to the command to halt was instant. He hit the brakes with such force that all three of them were almost thrown through the windscreen. But the assailant hung on. A bloody Dimitrov commissar, thought Richard. Still, better than a Moor. The commissar was bent on getting Richard's help in stopping men fleeing from the front. Shots were being fired over their heads to force them back. He was ordered out of the ambulance to assist. He leapt out, rifle at the ready, as did the machine gunner, but he had no ammunition. Richard was about to open fire towards figures pointed out to him in the semi-darkness when Joan rushed up and shouted above the uproar, "Put that thing away. That is not your job. Your job is to save this ambulance."

The order, and that's what it was, brought him to his senses even though he was pumped up with the fear of battle.

"What about the lads in the back?" he shouted.

"They're already out."

They both went round to the back of the ambulance to find the men in a tight group shielding behind it in a state of panic, not knowing what to do or where to go. Then their distress was heightened when, out of the darkness, three cavalrymen raced past them, their horses bolting in terror from the crashes and flashes of explosions. It was a scene of utter chaos, as close to a vision of hell as they would ever be likely to get.

"You've got to get away from here lads," yelled Richard. "We can't take you. We have to pick up wounded comrades." Pointing away from the front towards the left of the road, he indicated what he believed was the best direction. "I think that's the safest way. Best of luck."

And off they went at a good pace. Fortunately for them, the commissar had kept his attention focussed towards the front to stop those fleeing towards him, oblivious to the group of British lads who were retreating behind him. The commissar wouldn't have understood that far from desertion being in their minds, they were mainly concerned with finding their comrades. They didn't want to let them down.

"Now let us get out of here," urged Joan. Richard managed to turn the ambulance around without attracting the attention of the commissar and they got away from the commotion unnoticed. At some distance down the road, they picked up two wounded comrades who were greatly relieved to see an ambulance. They were told to lie down just in case it came under fire. Joan was as much concerned about the fierce Dimitrov as the enemy. He might well have thought that they too were fleeing, not simply trying to save the ambulance. But no shots pursued them. Perhaps he relented, she thought, having realised that they were non-combatants. They would never know and, in any case, they were both glad to get away. Once the wounded were lying down, she went back into the front. The situation was still tense, and she wanted to know what was happening. Nevertheless, further away from the action, she asked Richard to pull up so she could go in the back and check the wounded again. She gave them what treatment she could, reassured them that the firing they could still hear was now well behind them and returned to the cab. They proceeded slowly down the road, slowly because Richard wouldn't switch on the side lights, let alone the headlights.

They passed a few soldiers hobbling along then they came upon a group lying in the ditch. One of the soldiers stood up on recognising the ambulance and called out for assistance. Richard pulled up and Joan went over to them. They were Spanish. Three were badly wounded. Two were able-bodied and had decided to stay with their comrades rather than abandon them. They made themselves useful by helping to get the wounded onto stretchers and into the ambulance. The two who were already in the ambulance had to jam themselves up against the back of the cab; and to add further to the congestion, Joan decided to carry the two helpers as well. They will be able to look after the others when they are all off-loaded, she reasoned.

The prospect of being able to off-load their charges seemed to be a possibility when, a mile or two further on, they came across a lorry pulled off the road. They stopped. The Spanish driver explained that he could not get it started. Richard got into the driver's seat and tried the ignition but got no response.

"Joan, ask him if the battery's flat."

"He says it shouldn't be and he hasn't flattened it. He's just had no response from the ignition, like you."

She hoped he would get the lorry going. It was empty and she wanted to off-load the ambulance so as to be able to pick up other casualties. By now, the able-bodied soldiers were out of the back of the ambulance and grouped around the lorry's open bonnet. They offered one or two suggestions which Joan relayed, more out of courtesy to the would-be advisers than out of any belief that their suggestions would be any help to Richard. But they didn't know he was an experienced mechanic. The fault has got to be electrical, he thought. He was right. The contact points were burnt and not working. He removed them, polished them up and replaced them.

"Try now," said Joan, indicating to the driver to try the ignition. There was a response, so the fault had been found but, despite what the driver had said, the battery was almost flat. He must have flattened it after all, thought Richard.

"It's a push job Joan. Tell the driver to pull up as soon as he's got it going, so we can get him to take the wounded to the field hospital. He's sure to find it somewhere further back."

Fortunately there were enough of them to get it moving down the slight incline and after twenty or thirty yards the driver engaged gear and the engine leapt into life. He pulled up and moved into neutral. "*Gracias, gracias, gracias,*" the driver kept thanking them, relieved of his fear of being caught up in the Fascist advance. Taking all those who had been in the ambulance into the lorry, he was soon off down the road in search of the hospital.

"They must have re-established it further back by now, but how far back I can hardly guess. A lot will depend on someone's estimation of how long this breakthrough will continue and where it can be checked," Joan surmised as they returned to the ambulance.

Once back on the road they both realised how exhausted they were. They hadn't had much sleep for the last two nights and not much to eat either. The events of the day had drained them.

"We might as well stop here for what's left of the night," said Richard, pulling off the road and stopping under the cover of a large olive tree. "The action has died down and anyway there must be plenty of Republican comrades between us and the Fascists. We'll be safe enough."

After a simple meal, they settled down for the night. Exhausted as they both were, it wasn't easy to fall asleep with the adrenalin still running high. Uncertainty about the next day didn't help either. So Joan resorted to her unfailing way of allaying both their anxieties. It always worked. As they lay back on bunk and bench, she would ask some question about Richard's past. It might have been about life on Tyneside, about the Gateshead school or his life at sea.

"Your family were miners. Did you ever go down a mine yourself ? Did you ever go back to see the headmaster at the Gateshead school? Did you make friends with any Australians when you stopped at that Wallaroo place or any of the other places." She knew that he would never give a short answer when he could give a long one. And comforted by thinking of distant places, she would eventually fall asleep and when he became aware of that, he would soon follow, thinking he would tell her the rest of it in the morning.

*   *   *

At daybreak, they were woken up with the sound of aircraft and bombing, and decided to move out straight away. The Fascists were hammering the road and any other target they could find, and although the ambulance should have been recognisable for what it was from the air, there was no guarantee that their pilots would not target it. As they drove further from the front, they could still hear the sound of heavy guns. They wound the windows down to hear better the sound of aircraft, and when they did hear the characteristic drone, they either drove for the cover of trees if there were any, or stopped the ambulance in a skewed position off the road to make it look like an abandoned vehicle. They would hide in the ditch or behind a wall hoping to make themselves as inconspicuous as possible. Fortunately, aircraft come and go quickly and as soon as they disappeared from sight, they would set off again.

They passed through devastated *pueblos* abandoned by the locals escaping the bombing and the advancing front. They came to Hijar, another devastated *pueblo* devoid of citizens. It had recently been heavily bombed. Driving carefully through its empty debris-littered streets gave them a strange feeling. Particularly Joan. She had been there before during the Republican offensive the previous August. "The strange thing is," she said, "not only is there not much sign of life but there is not much sign of death."

"Not quite. Look over there." Richard pointed to the body of half a man, strangely hanging from a wire crossing high above the street. Both couldn't help wondering what had happened to the rest of him but neither of them voiced their thoughts.

They continued to crisscross the streets as best they could, avoiding those blocked by fallen buildings. Richard was in search of petrol, hoping that in the rush to get away not all the supplies had been used up. They stopped at intervals listening to hear any sounds of life. It paid off. At one intersection the clickety clack of someone operating a manual petrol pump echoed through the deserted town. "It's round the next corner," said Joan. "Don't drive round. Check out who's there first."

He jumped out and Joan handed him his rifle.

"Better take it, just in case," she said and watched as he crept warily towards the next corner, trying to avoid kicking bits of debris. The noise was getting louder and as he rounded the corner he saw two Americans filling up their lorry. They spotted him, and recognising him as a fellow Brigader gave a casual wave which he returned. He went back to the ambulance with the good news.

"They're Americans and there's petrol."

He drove round the corner and pulled in behind the lorry which was leaving just as they arrived.

"They weren't that friendly," said Joan.

"They just wanted to fill up and get away."

"That's what we should do, fill up and get away. This place is eerie. Once it was a thriving town. Now it's a chamber of horrors."

But he was filling up and wasn't really listening. "I feel better already," he said in a tone that was quite at odds with what Joan had said. "At least we have plenty of fuel. Let's get away from here and find somewhere to stop for the night."

After they had eaten and bunked down, he got in the first word for a change. He had tried before to get Joan to tell him about her family and the things she had done, believing that she must have had many interesting experiences. But she spoke again in the same self-deprecatory manner as before.

"Richard, I come from a boring middle class family, was sent to a boring boarding school to become a lady, horrified the family when I said I wanted to be a nurse, an occupation which they thought was only marginally superior to becoming a woman of the streets. And even nursing becomes boring after a while because of its deadening routine. So coming to Spain was a real challenge and I'm glad I came. After all I met you."

"Nursing couldn't have been so boring. After all you got into positions of authority, and your family couldn't be as boring as you say. You once told me that your cousin was a writer, a chap called Arthur Bryant and that he wrote history books and was well known."

"Well, that's true. I used to go to his house when I was a young girl, but I haven't seen him for years."

Joan gave no explanation of why she had lost contact with her well-known cousin. She knew that he was connected to the Conservative Party and had heard that he supported the Fascist cause in the Civil War. She kept that to herself. She admired his writing but did not agree with his politics. She often thought his position strange as so many writers and intellectuals, like Hemingway and Orwell, supported the Republican cause.

*   *   *

Next morning, after a quick cup of tea and stale bread dipped in olive oil, they decided to go west in the direction of the front hoping to re-establish contact with the Brigade. Soon they found their way blocked by columns of civilian refugees, hundreds coming towards them. There were vehicles in among them slowed down to little more than a walking pace. A few aircraft came overhead. The cry went up, "*Fascista! Fascista!*" The refugees went in all directions away from the road. This time they weren't Fascist aircraft, but the rush of the refugees from the road enabled them to get past the worst of the bottleneck. But they still had to slow down from time to time to carefully negotiate other groups. Further on they picked up two Spanish soldiers at the side of the road, one badly injured, the other attempting to look after him despite his own injuries. Joan's opinion was that the worst case needed surgical treatment beyond what she could do. His left leg was so badly smashed that it would have to be amputated. They put them both in the ambulance and turned back away from the front, in search of a transfer post. At one stage, they were going so slowly that some of the refugees managed to open the back of the ambulance and clamber inside thinking no doubt that it was a quicker way to safety. They both heard the commotion and decided it wasn't worth stopping to get them out. However two miles further on, Richard realised he had a puncture in a rear tyre. He pulled into the side quickly, jumped out, opened up the back and ordered them all out except for the badly injured one. They were all Spanish. Richard grabbed the spare wheel from the tray under the rear and loosened the nuts on the wheel with the puncture. But he didn't have to bother with the jack as the refugees lifted up the rear corner of the ambulance long enough for him to slip one wheel off and place the other one on. "*Gracias. Gracias*," he thanked them. Feeling appreciated, they were all for getting back into the ambulance but Joan insisted, "*Sólo para los heridos*." And they accepted that. Fortunately an empty supply lorry came along. Joan flagged it down and persuaded the driver to take on board all of those who had been in the ambulance. At her insistence he agreed to take the wounded soldier to a transfer post or hospital.

As they were already pulled off the road, they decided to stay in that position while more refugees passed. In among them this time were a few lorries and cars. Some distance from the ambulance one of the cars stopped and a tall figure got out and climbed on to the top of it. He stood, shading his eyes from the sun, and surveyed the scene in every direction. As he turned towards the ambulance, Richard recognised him. "It's Major Dunbar from the Fifteenth," said Richard, waving to him but he only got a slight nod of recognition in return. Dunbar was obviously preoccupied with the Fascist advance and what to do about it. He got back into the car and drove on past without giving them any further acknowledgement. It wasn't reassuring.

"It doesn't look good," said Joan, "if even he doesn't know what's going on."

* * *

They sat in the cab watching the last of the refugees straggle past. After they had all gone, they continued to stare through the windscreen still wondering about the significance of what they had seen. They had no knowledge of the broader scale of events. They felt cut off. Out of touch with the Brigade and unsure of the location of the nearest transfer post or hospital. Their mood of uncertainty wasn't helped by them not having had anything to eat or drink since early morning.

At last Richard broke the silence, "Let's have a cuppa and something to eat while we're deciding what to do next."

"Good idea." Joan was glad to break off thinking about the plight of the refugees.

The food and drink did something to lift their spirits but before they decided to go back towards the front or follow the path of the refugees they heard a vehicle coming towards them from the direction of the front. As it approached they recognised it as a Spanish staff car.

"Just what we need," said Joan, as she dashed out to flag it down. She explained their predicament to the officer in the car and he suggested that the best thing that they could do would be to bypass Caspe and report in at medical headquarters at Batea where he understood the Fifteenth Brigade had reassembled.

When thay reached Batea, they found medical headquarters housed in a large stone building. They reported in, said who they were and asked about the location of the Fifteenth Brigade. No one knew. Richard asked where he could get petrol and if he needed a permit. He was given one by the *tendencia* and directions to the pump which was at the end of a side road some distance away. He was asked to take a convalescing Brigader with him and drop him off at the food store for him to collect provisions, and then pick him up on the way back. They returned to the ambulance with the Brigader. He got up into the front next to Joan. She moved over to make room for him. He stank of sweat, garlic and wine but seemed sober enough. And they were used to foul odours. Comrades rescued from the front were often in a much worse condition, dirty and sweat-soaked and sometimes having soiled themselves with fear, thought Richard. But then we don't put them in the cab. It was just that he didn't like Joan being squashed up against him. But he is a Brigader, a volunteer fighting for the cause. He's probably been through hell.

They dropped him off at the stores and told him they'd soon be back to pick him up.

"Keep the windows down. Let's get a blow through," said Richard, as Joan moved back into the passenger's seat.

"When we pick him up, we'll put him in the back with the supplies."

"Yes. We can tell him to look after them," he said with a grin.

When they returned about fifteen minutes later, there was no sign of the Brigader. Richard switched off the motor and they both sat there waiting for him to come out. With the sun shining through the windscreen, Richard became drowsy and fell asleep. He's exhausted, thought Joan, getting more impatient. Finally, she decided to go into the stores to find out what was going on. She got out of the cab carefully so as not to wake him. A minute or so later, he twitched, slipped sideways in his seat and woke up with a start. Where's Joan, was his first thought, and then realising where he was, he knew she must have gone into the stores to find the Brigader. He jumped out intent on doing the same but at that very moment the Brigader appeared. He looked even more dishevelled than before and was now unsteady on his feet. He was clutching a large pumpkin and was being vigorously pushed in the direction of the ambulance by an angry Joan.

"He got into the *vino*," she shouted. "Let's get him back." The Brigader had staggered over to the ambulance and started clambering up into the cab. Richard, infuriated by his condition, grabbed him by the scruff of the neck, yanked him vigorously off the running board, frogmarched him to the back of the ambulance, threw him in and slammed the doors behind him. As they drove back, although angry herself, Joan became increasingly concerned by Richard's fury at what had happened. She tried to calm him but it didn't seem to work.

"We don't know what stress he's been under," she said.

"We've all been under stress," he hurled back.

"But he's a volunteer, not used to discipline."

"That's no excuse, we're all bloody volunteers."

"Yes, but you learnt discipline at that school and on the ships and so did I, as a nurse. We have had discipline drummed into us for years."

But he wouldn't listen. "There's no excuse for behaving like that."

The idea suddenly occurred to Joan that his seething anger might not be simply due to the Brigader's dereliction of responsibility, but at least partly due to the fact that he himself might be regarded as being responsible for the Brigader's behaviour and be seen as having let the side down. 'Not letting the side down' was deeply imprinted into Richard's psyche from the time he was at the reform school where if one person in a group did anything wrong, the whole group was punished. The odium of causing that was a powerful incentive to 'not let the side down'.

" Anyway, you're not to blame for what happened. We only dropped him off. It was his job to get the supplies, not yours."

But that didn't work either. When they arrived back at medical headquarters, Richard braked abruptly and saying nothing to Joan, ran round the back of the ambulance, flung open the doors, pulled out the Brigader by the legs and dumped him on the road like a sack of potatoes. That done, he strode into the building, and confronting the *tendencia* and a medical officer, screamed out, "Drunk and disorderly, dereliction of duty, ought to be court-martialled, deserves to be shot," along with a stream of curses. They both looked at Richard's performance with expressions of disbelief which abruptly changed to concern when he collapsed on to the floor. Joan, who had come up behind him, was as alarmed as they were.

The doctor started examining him.

"Does he have fits?" he asked Joan.

"Never, as far as I know."

"His breathing is fine but fast and his heart is beating like a drum. Now it's slowing down. He'll be O.K."

Joan explained what had happened as they placed him on a stretcher.

"I'll give him something that will knock him out for a few hours. Otherwise if he wakes up, all that agitation might start up again."

"He has never reacted like that before," she said. "We have been working the front since December at Teruel and he's a tough one. He was blown up at Brunete, and after recovering, insisted on going back in. He's a true believer."

"You sound like you are more than a little fond of him," said the doctor.

"If you are in an ambulance for twenty four hours a day for three months, you are likely to end up either detesting each other or ..." She didn't finish.

The doctor raised his eyebrows. "Is that a confession?"

Joan's stony glare made him realise that his question was inappropriate.

He didn't apologise but said in a brisk professional manner, "I'll keep him under observation here. Perhaps you'll take the opportunity to get some food while he's out to the world. You can't do anything for him at the moment."

9

CATALONIA

"What's happened? Where am I?"croaked Richard, heaving himself up. He was still on a stretcher but had been put in a room next to the one where he had collapsed. He cleared his throat and this time shouted out, "Anyone there?"

A Brigader rushed in. "So you're awake at last," he said.

"Where am I?"

"You're still here, guvnor, at medical headquarters." The Cockney accent and familiarity were reassuring.

 "How long have I been out?"

"Just overnight. The doctor gave you a shot so you could have a good long rest. He has recommended that you be given leave. Proper leave. Back to Blighty."

"Where's Joan then? Where is she?"

"You mean the nurse who was with you? Oh, she's been posted to a hospital further back. That's where we're all going. Further back, I mean. We're out on a limb here."

Only then did Richard become aware of the sounds of war. The familiar crump of shells some distance away made him realise that they were in a precarious position. The doctor hurried into the room. He was obviously pleased to see that Richard had woken up at last and seemed to be alert.

"You look a lot better this morning than yesterday afternoon," he said. " Stand up. Let's have a look at you." He tested his heart beat and blood pressure. "I think you'll do but I want you to stay around here for another day. Just in case. I've prepared a recommendation to Spanish Medical Aid in Barcelona that you be given leave to return to Britain. It documents your service on four battle fronts.Nurse Harrison told me all about that. Anyway your Brigader service book details where you've served. I don't think that with your credentials there will be any difficulty in you being granted leave. When you get to Barcelona, report to Mary Davison at Spanish Medical Aid. She'll sort things out. She'll need to get permission from the Spanish Army for you to leave Spain."

"So that's it!" exclaimed Richard, bewildered by the sudden turn of events. No Joan and back to Blighty, as the Cockney Brigader had put it.

"Yes, no ifs and buts," declared the doctor, handing him the letter to Spanish Medical Aid and a travel voucher. " You can leave tomorrow morning. Report to the military at Falset. They're in need of transport, so you will probably have company from there on. And don't worry about nurse Harrison, she'll be well behind the front by now. She might be lucky enough to be at the American hospital at Benicássim."

"Why lucky?"

"It's on the coast. Well away from the action." Then he added wistfully, "If I was ever to take up the government offer to the Internationals to live in Spain after the war, Benicássim would be the place for me. It's a beautiful spot."

Richard, now reassured about Joan, went outside to check that the ambulance was still where he had left it. It had to be, the keys were still in his pocket. Only Joan knew where he hid the spares under the bonnet. He went back inside for a morning cup of tea and dipped bread. It went down well, although he still preferred beef dripping to olive oil. Who wouldn't, he thought. But beggars can't be choosers.

Idleness never suited him so he spent the rest of the day checking out the ambulance. Three months of constant action showed both outside and in. He gave it as full a service as he could. Then he cleaned and tidied up the back and topped up the water, paraffin and meths containers. He thought Joan would be pleased with the way it looked by the time he'd finished.

✳   ✳   ✳

There was a fair bit of air activity on the journey to Falset but Richard was thankful that the road wasn't a target. When he reported in, he was told he had to proceed to Reus to pick up some wounded. Now an officer joined him in the front. Reus was being bombed when they arrived. They found the hospital and took the wounded into the ambulance as quickly as possible. He asked after Joan, but she wasn't there. He was ordered to take the wounded to Tarragona on the coast. He thought that it would be good to see the sea again and the green of the *huertas*. It was only a short journey to the coast and when he arrived at the hospital to off-load them, he was told to return to Reus to pick up another group. He asked after Joan again, but she wasn't there either. Fortunately, Reus was not being bombed when he returned, so he did not have to re-run the gauntlet. He picked up the additional wounded and returned to Tarragona as quickly as possible. There was no air activity but he knew that it could happen without warning. The Fascists seem to own the bloody skies, he thought.

At Tarragona, he handed over the Wales to the Spanish authorities. It had been his and Joan's home for the past three months. It had served them and the needs of hundreds of wounded comrades well. He also handed over his rifle, but decided to keep his treasured automatic until he got to Barcelona. He knew he wouldn't be able to travel armed through France. With one long last look at the Wales, he donned his Brigader - badged beret, picked up his rucksack and headed for the checkpoint on the road to Barcelona. There was no problem with getting a lift. There was plenty of traffic going there. He showed his papers to the soldiers at the checkpoint and then to the driver of one of the lorries. But he had to content himself with a lift in the back, joining the crowd. He wasn't used to that. The trip was uneventful, although they were at all times well within the range of Fascist aircraft. Barcelona had in fact been bombed since January. Perhaps as a response to the Republican victory at Teruel.

When he fronted up with his letter at Spanish Medical Aid, he was given a warm welcome. It was obvious he was expected and it seemed that the people there were aware of his contribution to the cause. Perhaps it was because of his record that they asked him if he would bring back to Barcelona another two ambulances which were being prepared in London. He agreed without hesitation. They knew he would. He had to wait two or three days in Barcelona. It wasn't a pleasant stay because of regular bombing by both German and Italian aircraft. The worst were the Italian bombers based in the Balearic Islands. They would drift in from the east and often catch the city unawares.

When approval came through from the Spanish authorities for him to leave, he handed over his automatic and left in their safe keeping all his papers except for his passport. On the day of his departure, he walked out of the office with only the clothes he was standing up in and his rucksack containing a few personal items; shaving equipment and the like. Every item of his clothing was worn out except his shoes. A Spanish worker in the medical office had noticed that his canvas shoes were falling apart, and thinking that Richard looked as if he wore about the same size as himself, offered him a spare pair of his own. They fitted well and were in good condition. Richard's thanks were met by the worker saying in broken English that he was grateful for the Brigaders coming to Spain.

"You gave us hope. The shoes are nothing."

10

BACK TO BLIGHTY

Getting out of Barcelona by air wasn't easy. The bombing was heavy and flights were frequently being cancelled, but eventually Richard got away at night, and much to his relief, landed safely in Marseilles. He went straight to the Thomas Cook's travel office to pick up his rail and boat tickets to London. He expected them to be waiting for him. They weren't, and the Cook's people knew nothing about him. All he could do was book into a *pension*, boarding house, and go back the following day. Next morning on his return to Cook's, the situation was just the same. They had received no notification from either Barcelona or London. He then had the idea that the Communist Party authorities in Marseilles might be prepared to help him, seeing that he was a Party member. But they treated his story with great suspicion as he couldn't produce his Brigade service book. They thought he was a deserter.

There were plenty of deserters now that the Fascists seemed to be gaining the upper hand. Marseilles Communist Party authorities knew well that the commissars' attitude towards deserters in Spain was unforgiving. And so was theirs. Richard was becoming desperate. The idea that anyone would think of him as a deserter added to his frustration at not being able to do anything about his plight. He was always able to cope, always able to think through a situation and always prepared to act. But now it was as if he was wandering in limbo with only a passport to identify himself. And that was all it did. So he returned to the *pension*, thinking that all he could do would be to try again next day. In the morning, Cook's gave him the same response as the day before. "We have not received anything, sir." A further visit to the Communist Party office at least gave indications that they now believed his story, so vehemently did he tell them what he had done in Spain. But still they were not prepared to help, except that they did suggest he might try the British Consul. He took the advice, only to find the Consul also unwelcoming. Britain's non-intervention policy led British officials to look unkindly on those who had volunteered to assist the Republican cause in Spain.. Richard's despair, and possibly the fact that he was a non-combatant led the Consul to relent. He said he would make inquiries, gave him a few francs and suggested he book in at the Seaman's Mission. Staying at the Mission was another British Brigader. Despite his own recent experiences, Richard did suspect that this young lad really was a deserter. There was something about his manner. A certain furtiveness. Now was not the time to be judged guilty by association, so Richard kept his distance. A day later, a message came through to the Mission for him to go to Cook's. The Consul's inquiries had worked. Everything was arranged and he was given train and boat tickets for London.

*   *   *

When Richard boarded the Paris train, he felt an enormous sense of relief at being released from the prison without bars that Marseilles had become. It was early spring, and as the train sped through the Rhône Valley, the scenery was lush and green. Vineyards and corn-

157

fields separated by rows of poplars. So different from the barrenness of the Meseta and the frightful snows of Teruel. And the bustling towns and picturesque villages, so different from the shattered wrecks of Aragón. It all seemed so utterly unreal. A dream replacing a nightmare.

At the Gare de Lyons in Paris, he had barely stepped from the carriage to the platform when a complete stranger threw his arms around him in a great bear hug. "Brigader, Brigader!" he shouted as if declaring to the whole of Paris what he had found. Richard was overwhelmed by this reception and could offer no resistance to being led to a shoe-shine boy in the main concourse of the railway station. While his shoes were being polished the Frenchman conveyed that his name was Maurice. Richard showed him his ticket to Dieppe because he didn't know how to get to the Gare St. Lazare. Maurice explained that he would have to travel by the Metro, the Paris underground. Noticing that there was a big time gap before the Dieppe train left, Maurice insisted on taking Richard for a meal. He led him to a cafe across the street from the station. All this time Maurice, who was dressed in workman's clothes, spoke to Richard in a torrent of French, out of which only words such as 'liberté, démocratie, and camarade' were clear to him. Although bewildered by all this, he recognised that the welcome was genuine.

As they entered the cafe they were engulfed in cheering. Never before had Richard experienced people wanting to shake his hand or slap him on the back. They cleared a place for the two of them at a table, and in no time the *plat du jour* and tumblers of *vin rouge* were placed in front of them. They were eager for news from Spain. "Where had he been? Jarama, Madrid, Brunete, Teruel?" A collective gasp went up each time he nodded. "Teruel, Teruel," said one across the table, shaking his head. He knew well what had happened there. A great Republican victory followed by a rout. The blizzards and the frostbite had all been reported in the French press. "Let him eat. Let him eat," implored his new found friend. It was fish soup. And they did, drawing satisfaction from Richard's obvious enjoyment of the best meal he'd had in months. And drew satisfaction too from their own identification with the cause, through their acclamation of a Brigader who'd been in the thick of it.

Soon after they had finished eating, Maurice indicated that it was time to go and that he would go with him on the Metro. They left the cafe to shouts of *"Bon voyage!"* and *"Adieu!"*

The journey to Dieppe and across the Channel to Folkestone and London passed quickly, helped by him falling asleep twice on the train, in France and in England. It must be the food and the wine he thought. But the fact that he was physically and mentally exhausted had a lot to do with it. When he was awake, he wondered where Joan was. If she is in a hospital, she should be safe, he thought, they're a fair way behind the lines.

*   *   *

It was late in the day when he arrived in London, and because of the time he went straight to his mother's house in Finsbury Park. When she opened the door, the look of relief on her face was the best of welcomes. British press reports on the progress of the war had told her that the Republicans were in retreat. She hadn't been sure whether he was dead or alive, not having heard anything of him for months. He was also given a great welcome by his stepfather. It made him think of his own father whom he could hardly remember. Just that dim recollection of being ushered into a darkened room and kissing him, and then being ushered out. His father had died the next day. But this was no time for sadness. In no time at all, his step-father had been to the off-licence and brought back bottles of beer to celebrate the home-coming.

"I'm not used to this you know. It's all wine in Spain, '*tinto or blanco*'. This is my first beer in months!"

"It will go down all the better for that," said his mother.

"It does an' all," he responded, playing up his Geordie accent.

He didn't tell his mother about Joan. His mother knew he had been walking out with a girl from South Shields, Elsie Dunn. Before he became involved with Joan, he had written regularly to Elsie and was glad to get letters back. He had even sent his sister money to buy Elsie a birthday present. Once a fellow Brigader from South Shields fronted up to him in Teruel. He had been told by Elsie's father that Richard was working on the ambulances and that he should look out for him. They had both been glad to see someone from home and to talk about people and places they both knew well, even though they hadn't known each other before. It was hard not to feel guilty about dropping Elsie and about not even telling her.

Next day he took the bus into the city and went straight to Spanish Medical Aid. He was told the two ambulances would be ready for delivery in two days time. Another driver was available for the second ambulance and there would be one other passenger who would be responsible for meals and accommodation en route and for any other administrative matters.

Richard's mother was dismayed that he was only home for a short stay, but at least she could comfort herself with the thought that as a non-combatant, he would almost certainly return. Of course she knew nothing of the type of war Franco and his German and Italian allies were waging. Had she, there would have been no peace of mind.

1

BARCELONA

By a curious stroke of circumstance, the passenger in charge of the ambulance delivery was none other than Ted Fletcher who had been with Richard on the previous delivery. They had seen each other quite a few times in Spain. Now they enjoyed sharing their experiences in the cabin of the lead ambulance as they made their way to Dover, through France and across the Spanish border to Barcelona. Both were keen to get there. Fletcher knew his organisational skills would be needed by the Fifteenth Brigade and Richard wanted to find Joan and get back to ambulance duties.

The bombing of Barcelona had continued during his absence and shattered and burnt out buildings were everywhere. The sight of it all raised his concerns for Joan. When they arrived at Spanish Medical Aid headquarters, Fletcher went inside to formally hand over the two ambulances. Richard followed and was astounded by the number of people in the offices, some in nurses' uniform and others in military uniform. When he had left only two or three weeks before, it had seemed a much more civilian operation.

The building was a maze of rooms, mostly small. He went from one to another looking for someone he knew who could tell him what was going on. But he didn't have much success. They were either too busy or too reluctant to provide information to someone they barely knew or they couldn't speak English. And the latter could be a useful excuse. It was late afternoon and after getting himself a bite to eat at the makeshift cafeteria accompanied by a glass or two of *vino*, a great weariness came over him. He had been on the go since he had left the Figueres army base that morning, and apart from the long drive itself, there was the added tension and concern during the drive south that they might be targeted by Italian aircraft swooping in from the east.

At least he got an answer to the question of where he could bed down. In a large empty room. No beds, not even carpet, just floor boards. Dropping his rucksack in a corner for use as a pillow, he was sound asleep in no time. It would have taken a direct hit to wake him up, that's if it didn't put him to sleep forever.

When he did wake up, he found himself in a crowded dormitory filled with comrades including one or two women, all sleeping in their day clothes. At the cafeteria they fixed him up with a coffee and some bread and sausage. Must be dead donkey laced with gar-lic, he thought, but at least the bread was good. After that he set out on rounds of the building in search of news. He hadn't gone far down the main corridor when he heard his name called out in an authoritative voice. Is that me, he thought. Again "Richard," rang out, and he turned to find it was Fred Copeman, the British Battalion commander calling him.

"I heard you were back. I've got a job for you."

"Yes, sir," he replied, pleased at last to find someone who could bring him up to date, and who better than Copeman. He was eager

163

to get back on the job and also flattered to have been sought after by the commander himself. "Where's the Battalion, sir?" he blurted out, before Copeman had a chance to tell him about the job he wanted him to do. He presumed it would be back at the front on ambulance duty. After all, that was what he was there for.

Copeman looked gravely at him. Only recently released from hospital, his face was drawn and although his eyes still had that customary penetrating gaze, there was something different. "You obviously don't know what's been happening. The Brigade has taken heavy casualties. Merriman and Tapsell have been killed along with many others. They were overrun and many were taken prisoner. God knows what's happened to them."

"Where's Joan then?" interrupted Richard, his tone and expression betraying his anxiety.

"She's alright," said Copeman, not minding the interruption. He knew that Richard and Joan were together and he had a lot of time for Joan as she had nursed him after Teruel. "I had her brought into Barcelona. There's plenty of work here with all the bombing." A flicker of a smile crossed his face when he saw Richard's obvious expression of relief. "She's staying in a hotel only a few blocks away. You can go and catch up with her when I've told you about the job."

He had almost forgotten about the job, his mind being filled with the disaster that had struck the Brigade, what Franco's Moors might do to the prisoners and the knowledge of Joan's safety. The cocktail of emotions made it difficult for him to return to the issue of the job.

"I have a report that I want you to take back to London, to Communist Party Headquarters in King Street. Commissar Bill Rust is here in Barcelona and he agrees with me that the report is best delivered by hand. It's just too sensitive to be sent by wireless. We don't want the information it contains falling into the wrong hands."

"But I want to get back to the Brigade."

Copeman knew that he was committed otherwise he wouldn't have come back. He also knew he could be relied on. "Richard, this is an important assignment, and I trust you to do it. Go and see Joan now, and I would like to see both of you in the morning."

"Thank you, sir."

Richard left, somewhat bewildered by the turn of events but looking forward to seeing Joan. Bombs were falling somewhere in the city but fortunately the area between the Spanish Medical Aid building and the hotel was not under attack and it wasn't far.

Joan was in the hotel sitting room and was startled to have her name called out. She instantly knew the voice and almost jumped out of the armchair in which she had been half reading, half dozing. The relief so visibly displayed at being together again was a common enough sight in a city which was being relentlessly bombed, and loved ones often separated at the time of the attacks. Their embrace ended with him gently holding Joan by the shoulders. From his expression she knew he was disturbed by something.

"They want me to go back to London straight away," he said.

"Who's they?"

"Fred Copeman. But I want to stay here with you. There's lots in need of medical aid now. The lads at the front and with all this bombing, Spanish civilians as well."

"I don't think we should be talking about what Copeman wants you to do here. We've been warned about loose talk and spies. Let's go up to my room and we can talk in private."

Joan had caused Richard to feel guilty about using the name of the British Battalion commander in a public place. Things had obviously changed, he thought. He had assumed that he was among pro-Republicans, but with the bombing there were now many waverers, not to mention Franco's vaunted fifth-columnists.

The room was sparsely furnished. A bed and a small cupboard. Fading wallpaper and an unshaded light bulb hanging from the ceiling giving it the appearance of a prison cell. Despite the ambience, they embraced again. They hadn't been together since his blackout in Aragón.

"How long have you been here in Barcelona?" he asked.

"Just a few days. When the Brigade was overrun, we were pulled out. We were lucky not to be taken prisoners as so many were. They didn't stand a chance. Constant shelling, tank attacks, and wave after wave of bombers and fighters. We had the men but they had the machines."

"We've got Germany and Italy to thank for that."

"More so Britain, perfidious Albion, with its farce of non-intervention forcing the Spanish Government to rely on Russia for arms. Anyway, let's not go over that again. It's too depressing. What is it that Copeman wants you to do?"

"He wants me to go to London more or less straight away. He has prepared a report that he wants delivered by hand to King Street."

"It probably tells it as it is, without the gloss."

"What do you mean?"

"It's probably a report on how grave the situation really is, and because of that he doesn't want to risk sending it by wireless even in code."

"It sounds important but why me?"

"You're a non-combatant," replied Joan emphatically. "Who'd think an ambulance driver would be trusted with such an important message? And anyway, trust is the name of the game. Who else would leave a war like this and voluntarily return like you've just done?"

"But we're all volunteers, Joan."

"Yes, but you came back, at a time when things are going bad. Many wouldn't have."

Richard lapsed into silence. He thought to himself that he would come back again and again as long as Joan was still in Spain. He couldn't just leave her there, and he still believed in the cause. But now he was back, he didn't want to leave. At last he said, "Well, Copeman wants to see both of us first thing tomorrow."

"Now you tell me. So I'm involved too. It sounds to me that he wants to make doubly sure his message gets through."

"He didn't say that to me," responded Richard.

"No, but I suspect he thinks of us as a team."

*   *   *

Next morning at Spanish Medical Aid, they found Copeman in an office working through papers. Pinned on the wall behind him, were maps of Aragón and Catalonia. On them thick lines and arrows marked the course of battle. He casually beckoned them to come in and sit down, conveying the impression that he was expecting them.

"The situation is desperate," he said. "The Fascists have cut through to the Mediterranean at Vinaroz, and so the Republic is now cut in two. It could be worse. We still hold Madrid, Valencia and Barcelona, but the future's bleak."

He paused for a moment, looking directly at them. "I want you both to go back to England. Your war is over. You've done enough. And Richard, I want you to hand deliver my report. It will be your final act of service. I'll obtain the travel papers and make transport arrangements. I will get you to the French border . I know if I get you that far, you will do the rest. It's too risky trying to fly out with the city and airport being continuously bombed."

Richard and Joan just sat there speechless. Copeman had made the decision for them. There was no room for negotiation. Copeman was in command. He always was. He could plainly see from their expressions that they didn't seem pleased at the prospect of leaving Spain. He suspected their concern was about who would provide medical support to the Brigade. After a long silence, he said, "Don't worry about the Brigade and the Battalion. They are being regrouped on this side of the Ebro. They are in the Spanish army now, and its medical support is excellent. Joan reflected on his last comment. She knew that it wasn't just said to placate them. She knew that the war had seen major advances by the Spanish medical service in the treatment of the wounded; surgery as immediate as possible, blood transfusions in the field, fractures immobilised with

Plaster of Paris. She believed medical support was a priority in an army of equals, and that soldiers should not be treated as disposable items as they had been in the Great War.

"Be ready to leave first thing tomorrow. I'll get the paper work speeded up. You had both better bunk down here tonight just in case there's any change of plan. So go and enjoy your last day in Barcelona." His last words were drowned out by explosions which shook the building. "That was too close for comfort," he added with a grim smile. "Take care."

Walking away down the corridor, Richard muttered, "So that's it!"

"Yes, that's it!" responded Joan, and that was all they said for a long time.

*   *   *

They were up soon after daybreak and packed their belongings, Richard into his treasured rucksack and Joan into a large shoulder bag. Not that they had much. They left their baggage in the corner of the room that had served as a dormitory and went down to the cafeteria to get something to eat. Soon the sounds of movement in the building increased, and with breakfast finished, they sought out Copeman. He was talking in the corridor to the Spanish driver who was to take them to the French frontier. Together they checked that all the paperwork was complete; authorisation to travel, petrol vouchers, and for Richard and Joan, passports, rail and boat tickets to take them to London.

Copeman sat in the front of the staff car with the driver, propping his light machine gun on his right side against the door of the car. All four were silent as the car wound its way through the shattered streets. Once out of the city, their progress was slowed down by groups of refugees, mainly older men, women and children, carrying whatever they could of their belongings on their backs or in prams and carts, all making their way to the safety of France. They had endured the bombing for more than three months but being overrun by Moors was an even more terrifying prospect. From time to time, when an aircraft appeared overhead, the refugees would dive for the ditches uncertain as to whether the aircraft were '*nuestros*' or '*Fascistas*'. And when the skies were clear, the sorry slow procession would start again.

All the time, the four in the staff car sat solemnly, anguished at the Spanish exodus. In the strictest sense, most were not Spanish at all. They were Catalán. They spoke their own language and had their own customs and culture. Because of their spirit of independence and separateness, they were particularly fearful of what would befall them if Franco took Catalonia. They knew he saw it as a hotbed of communists, socialists and anarchists.

By the time they were half way to the frontier, the stream of refugees had dwindled. The atmosphere in the car became less tense particularly as the risk of air attack diminished. Richard found the confidence to break the silence. "Sir, what happened to the Brigade, how did we get overrun?"

Copeman said nothing in response for some time, and Richard was beginning to wonder if he had been heard. Should he repeat it? Was he being deliberately ignored? Had he done the wrong thing in asking? Had he the right to ask the British Battalion commander such a blunt question? After what seemed an interminable lapse of time, Copeman, half turning towards the driver so as to better direct his voice to the back, said quietly, "The Fascist firepower was over-whelming. A retreat had been ordered, but great confusion was created when a number of Fascist light tanks somehow tricked the Battalion into thinking they were Republican. All hell was let loose. The Brigade was cut off. Many Brigaders were either killed, wounded or taken prisoner as they went in the wrong direction. And that's how Merriman and Tapsell got killed."

Copeman's despondency was fed by the fact that he hadn't been there. He had sufficient faith in himself as a commander to believe he could have made a difference. However, he had been too ill at the time to be in the field, and he tried not to take solace from his recognition that now the tables had turned, such defeats at the front were inevitable for as long as the war was pursued. The report he was asking Richard to deliver provided that grim assessment. The war had become unwinnable.

There wasn't much more conversation. They were for the most part lost in their own thoughts. It was April and the landscape was tinged with green from the winter rains. Wheatfields, vineyards and olive groves all full of promise, and towering above them the forested sierras. Had it not been for the refugees straggling north, they could have enjoyed that scenic feast to the full. But they were faced not merely with the reality of the present, but with the realities of the past and the future.

At Figueres, they called into the Republican army base as required, to get their papers checked and be given clearance to leave Spain. As they got close to the border post, Copeman turned to Richard and handed over his report. It was in a small envelope. It could in fact have easily been taken for just an ordinary letter. "Now that must be delivered by you to the Senior Executive of the Communist Party at King Street. You have been there, so you know exactly where I mean. It must not fall into the hands of other people including the border guards ahead. So where are you going to put it?"

"In my shoe, it will be safe there."

"Good," said Copeman, "And there's something else." He handed a brown paper parcel over into the back. "It's a football signed by just about everyone in the Battalion. I want you to deliver this to King Street as well, for safe keeping."

Richard took the ball carefully. A sacred object. He could not avoid thinking that for some of the lads all that might come back from the war would be their signatures.

As the car was not crossing the border, the driver stopped before the checkpoint. They all got out except the driver and came round to the front. Copeman gave Joan an unmilitary hug, and Richard a firm handshake. Both were visibly distressed to be leaving knowing well that the war was continuing, and Spanish and Brigader comrades would still be in need of medical support

"Farewell, brave souls, you have done everything required of you. If only ..." but he tailed off. With that Copeman walked briskly back to the staff car, gave one last wave and was soon disappearing down the road back to the war. They turned to each other, sad-eyed but saying nothing and together walked reluctantly towards the border post.

*   *   *

Crossing into France was straight forward. They weren't even searched. Not even asked about the parcel. They weren't expected to have anything worth searching for. An April train journey through the lush Rhône Valley, and the fertile grain fields of the Paris basin should have gladdened their hearts. Life replacing death. But it didn't. Their thoughts were with those they had left behind and those who would never return. Whenever they stopped on the journey, they were overwhelmed by the array of fruit, vegetables, cheeses and sausages set out in shops or on stalls, but they had no stomach for it. It was as if they felt guilty at the idea of gorging themselves when they knew the Battalion would be on iron rations. And their conversation was sparse. When they looked out of the carriage window each imagined the other was thinking the same; that last battle, the killing, the maiming, the prisoners and not being there. An unspoken conspiracy of silence. They showed little awareness of other travellers who, recognising them as Brigaders, averted their eyes as if to distance themselves from their look of defeat. After all the reports of Franco's recent advances, most suspected the Republican cause was lost so there was no longer vicarious glory to be had by association with Brigaders.

12

LONDON

It was late in the evening when they arrived in London. They went straight by bus to Richard's mother's at Finsbury Park.

"I don't know what she'll think about me bringing you home," said Richard in an uncertain voice.

"Well, we are about to find out," replied Joan. But she was anxious, as she knew his real father had died when he was a young boy and his mother had remarried. Would his step-father welcome her as readily as he had welcomed Richard? Any doubts she had were swept away. No sooner had he introduced her and somehow managed to convey that they were together, mostly by expression, than she was given a daughter's welcome. In a matter of minutes they were lifted from the slough of despond they had been in since leaving Spain.

Next morning Richard left Joan with his mother and took the bus into the city. His first mission was to go to King Street and hand in Copeman's report and the parcel containing the autographed football. He was pleased that Joan was getting on so well with his mother. She had decided to stay home so they could get to know each other better. He felt strange on the crowded bus. Here I am, he thought, on the top deck of a red London bus looking out over the busy streets of the city listening to the bustle of traffic, when only a few days ago I was looking at the shattered and burnt out buildings of another city, listening to the sound of exploding bombs. Londoners had escaped the possibility of that by their government appeasing Hitler. It, in collusion with France, had delivered Spain to Franco. He was so lost in such thoughts that when the bus got to his stop he dashed to get off leaving the football behind.

The doorman at the Communist Party headquarters let him through when he had stated his business. He was directed to a room where five or six glum-faced men were having a meeting. They looked up eyeing this unknown intruder. Before any of them could speak, Richard blurted out, "I have a letter from the British Battalion commander, Fred Copeman. He asked me to hand deliver it to Senior Executive."

One of them reached out and took the letter from him with a sombre, "Who are you then?"

Richard gave his name and explained who he was and how his ambulance role for Spanish Medical Aid in support of the Fifteenth Brigade and the Battalion had led to Copeman and other officers making use of him from time to time, and that he was in the Party. They nodded an unsmiling acceptance of his explanation and the one holding the letter simply said, "Alright, you can go." No 'thank you'. No expression of appreciation for his contribution to the cause. So that's it, he thought. Fourteen months and not even a thank you from the very people who wanted me to go. He left the building promptly and went round to Spanish Medical Aid to tell them that the two ambulances and their contents had been delivered unscathed to Barcelona. At least there they thanked him and asked him how it was. So he went home in a more cheerful frame of mind.

*   *   *

It must have been a week later that it dawned on him that he had not handed in the football. He felt bad about that. He felt he had let the lads down and Copeman.

"Why did I have to muck it up at the end?"

"Stop it," implored Joan. "It was only a football, and the lads will be remembered in more important ways."

"Well, let's hope they are, but they'll never be able to go back to Spain, like was promised. The Republican Government said they could even come back and live there if they wanted to when the war was won."

"Yes, I know," said Joan, joining in Richard's melancholy, "that will never happen now. The Brigaders will never be able to even visit Spain, let alone live there."

SIXTY ONE YEARS

13

ENGLAND
1938

Richard and Joan stayed with his mother and step-father for three weeks, then they caught the train to Newcastle to visit his aunt Ethel and uncle George at Marsden and all his other relatives who lived on Tyneside. They were made very welcome everywhere and Joan, with her posh southern accent, was treated as something of a celebrity. Language problems were a source of fun as she tried to cope with their Geordie accents, and they with hers. The only sour note was from the Dunn family who, when they saw Richard out with Joan, felt that their Elsie had been badly treated.

While staying with aunt Ethel, they got married officially at the local registry office as their Alcorisa marriage could not be recognised in Britain. Richard found work driving a tip truck for a sand and metal firm and now, with a regular wage coming in, they decided to rent a terrace house in South Shields. Joan went round the second hand furniture shops and with her authoritative manner and accent was able to convince the salesmen of the true value of the items she wished to purchase. However, after a few months of poor weather, they decided to return to the London area, and at first stayed with his mother's sister, Mary, at Enfield. She was not only able to put them up in the spare room but also able to take in their best items of furniture which they arranged to be sent by removals. Richard soon got a job in Enfield driving an elderly couple, the Wades, who were semi-retired but still owned a tailoring business with several retail outlets. He would drive them from their home to their different shops and occasionally to Frinton where he would leave them at their holiday house to be collected on a designated date. All the time he worked for them he had access to their Sunbeam car which he looked after and serviced. He also did gardening and other odd jobs for them at their large Enfield house.While he was driving for the Wades, Joan worked as a visiting nurse in the area looking after the health needs of elderly people and sick children in their own homes.

After being with the Wades for three months, the foreman of Earnshaw's found out that Richard was back in the London area. He came to see him to tell him that there was a job going, and that if he wanted it, he would try and find them a place to live in Welwyn Garden City. He had fond memories of working for the Earnshaws. Capitalist Socialists, Joan had jokingly called them. The foreman was true to his word. He found them a house. Richard handed in his notice to the Wades and they moved to Welwyn Garden City, delighted to have a place of their own. And Joan soon found a job at the local hospital.

The Spanish Civil War was still going on during this time. The International Brigades were withdrawn in September 1938. It was a cause lost, but the war dragged on until April 1939. Franco took Barcelona in January, but not until March was he able to take Madrid. By this time the German Fascists were making history elsewhere. In March 1938 Hitler annexed Austria. However, German troops were apparently welcomed by many if not most Austrians. Then, disregarding British Prime Minister Chamberlain's appeasing Munich Agreement, which allowed Germany to occupy only the Sudetenland area of Czechoslovakia, German troops entered Prague in March 1939. In September 1939 they invaded Poland. Britain delivered an ultimatum to Hitler. It was ignored. To honour a six month old guarantee given to Poland, a state of war between Britain and Germany automatically followed.

At this turn of events, Richard was further convinced that he was right to have supported the struggle against fascism in Spain. He was prouder than ever of having been a Brigader, and in 1939 he and Joan went to a large International Brigades' reunion in London's Empress Hall. It was the nearest thing to a thanks that they were ever to receive in England.

With the outbreak of war, Britain started a military call-up. Richard went to the Merchant Navy Recruitment Office to volunteer for that service. Details of his previous service on trading ships were recorded by the recruiting officer who told him that they would be in touch. He returned home confident of being called up. But months passed and nothing happened.

While waiting for the call-up, he had to leave Earnshaw's as the noxious nature of its activities forced the factory to be relocated. He moved to a new job at Hatfield. The firm, Jack Olding, was the British distributor for the U.S.A. Caterpillar company which manufactured tractors and heavy earth - moving equipment. The job involved servicing and driving the vehicles. After some time there, a position in Persia was advertised by the construction firm Balfour & Beatty, training locals in the use of heavy earth-moving equipment. He applied and was accepted by them but then received a letter stating that the Government had refused his application to leave the country. No reason was given. He could only assume that it was because he had been a Brigader, and more significantly, was on record as having been a member of the Communist Party. He also thought that the same reasons explained why he hadn't been called up into the merchant navy. That he had ceased to be a Party member only served to heighten his frustration.

In 1940, Joan gave birth to their first child, a daughter they named Evelyn, and in 1941, a son they named Duncan Tapsell; Tapsell after commissar Walter Tapsell who had married them at Alcorisa in Spain and had been killed in Aragón. This meant that during the entire period of the war Joan was busy rearing their two young children, but there was still other work to be done for which she was well qualified. With the German bombing of London and industrial cities, many children were evacuated to country retreats. Novelist J.B. Priestley opened his country estate in Herefordshire for that purpose, and Joan took Evelyn and Duncan there for their safety, but also to care for the needs of other children at the same time. In May 1941, the Germans broke off the bombing campaign, the Blitz as it was called by Londoners, to concentrate efforts on the invasion of Russia. The Blitz had cost Britain 30,000 lives, mostly civilian, but had proved costly to Germany in loss of aircraft and air crew. Returning to Welwyn Garden City from the country, Joan worked for a time at a local day care centre, again caring for children including her own.

Richard's work at Olding's took on a military character as the firm became involved in collecting Canadian and American tanks from various ports around Britain, fuelling and servicing them, then driving them onto railway low-loaders for transport to Hatfield. Some of the ships carrying the tanks across the Atlantic also carried a cargo of wheat in which the tanks were actually buried. At port, the wheat had to be removed first before the tanks could be craned from the holds. At Hatfield the tanks were further serviced and made battle ready. Then they were driven to tank parks in wooded areas where they were well camouflaged from the air. Invasion of Europe was planned but still in the future.

The first tanks to arrive were the Canadian Rams and the American General Lees and General Grants. In 1942 these were superseded by the American Sherman tank which became the main battle tank for the allied campaigns in North Africa and Europe. 40,000 Sherman tanks were to be built and were first used in action by the British at El Alamein in North Africa. The Rams never saw battle. They were used for crew training. All the tanks were lever-steered which meant that to change direction, one track had to be slowed, disengaged or locked.

One day, Richard was told to drive a tank with a colleague to Woolwich Arsenal for special testing. When they arrived, they drove the tank onto a parade ground. The colleague who was in the turret saw that they had caused a commotion bringing the tank onto that hallowed surface.

"Get out of here before we're court martialled," he shouted to Richard, above the roar of the engines. This prompted him to lock one track, turn the tank through 180 degrees, and make off at top speed, churning up the tarmac in the process.

"Well, if they hadn't scared the wits out of us, it wouldn't have happened," said Richard afterwards. "Anyway, we're civilians, so they can't court martial us!"

They proceeded further down the road, glad to turn a corner and be out of sight of the damaged parade ground. They were waved over to stop outside a large building where there was a group of people looking incongruous in civilian clothes. They were both expecting the army. They got out of the tank and were told to stand well away from it. Then a white-coated bespectacled fellow came out of the building. He was carrying a rifle, and large sheets of white paper. He entered the tank and stuck sheets of paper all round the inside of it and also trapped one sheet on the inside of the door. By now, all the other civilians had retreated some distance from the tank, obviously knowing what was going to happen next. The fellow with the rifle, taking careful aim, fired several shots at the door, or more specifically, at the edge of the door.

"What's all this about?" asked Richard of one of the civilians.

"Reports from North Africa are that when shrapnel or bullets strike the door when this tank is in action, fine splinters penetrate and ricochet around inside, causing injury to the crews. Some poor blighters have been hit in the eye. So we're trying to replicate that phenomenon here," was the somewhat haughty response.

The white-coated fellow handed the rifle to one of the others and went back into the tank, collecting all the sheets of paper. He came out smiling grimly and nodding his head. The sheets were perforated. The doors were inadequate.

Working with tanks throughout 1942, 1943 and much of 1944, led to Richard becoming expert in handling them. But there were tricky moments. Driving them off ships down steep ramps was one of them because at the point of entry onto the ramp, he would be driving blind, looking into mid-air, relying on others to signal to him that his alignment was alright. The thought of being in a tank falling off the ramp onto the wharf below was enough to put fear into anyone. On one occasion, the sequence was in reverse. The plan was to test the feasiblity of carrying invasion tanks as deck cargo. This time, he had to drive the tank up the ramp to the far side of the deck where it was to be turned on the turn-table through 90 degrees for parking on the side decks. Others would follow. The turn-table proved to be not quite large enough for the tank to be turned. He was urged to go further forward, but at the point where the tank was partly hanging over the side of the vessel and he could see water and barges below, he was sure that any further movement forward would have had him toppling into the harbour. He had the measure of the tank. It wasn't going to work. Then he had to reverse it back across the deck and down the ramp to the wharf. He didn't want to try that again and was glad he wasn't asked to.

✳   ✳   ✳

Towards the end of 1944 when the allied invasion of France was in full swing, Richard was at last called up for military service. Curiously, given his wartime experience at Olding's, he was offered work in the mines or the forces. He asked for the Navy and was given the Army. After basic training, he was put in the Royal Engineers for further training which involved building Bailey bridges and mine detection and clearance. Halfway through the course, he was interviewed for a position training instructors on handling earth-moving equipment and tanks modified for obstacle clearance. The plan was for them to then train others attached to fighting units in Europe. Much to the annoyance of those running the Royal Engineers' course, he was transferred to the School of Mechanical Equipment at Ripon in Yorkshire to become an instructor himself. The course lasted several weeks, and twelve would-be trainers were instructed in earth moving and tank handling skills. A Tank Corps instructor assisted him, using six tanks modified for obstacle removal. The turrets and guns had been taken off and they had been fitted with bulldozer blades. Richard, who was supervisor for the course, was congratulated by senior staff at the school on its success. The skills and satisfaction he had gained from that instructing role were to point the way to new opportunities after the war.

14

PALESTINE AND IRAQ
1946

Richard remained in the Army until April 1946, working mainly on tanks. With the European war over in May 1945, he had been able to get leave regularly to go home to Joan and the family. But the children were used to their father not being there day after day as were the children of many other families during the war. The abnormal was normal. And so, when he left for the Middle East a month after he was demobbed, Evelyn and Duncan would have thought there was nothing unusual about it, while Joan herself had become accustomed to his absences. At least she wasn't a widow as many others had become.

Construction company, John Howard, had a contract with the Iraq Petroleum Company to build a second and larger capacity oil pipeline parallelling the existing one from Kirkuk in northern Iraq to Haifa on the Mediterranean coast. The company had advertised a position to train local Arab workmen in the use of heavy earth - moving and trenching equipment. Richard applied and got the job. Along with seventeen other John Howard employees, he boarded the Queen Elizabeth for Port Said and Ismailia, a port half way along the Suez Canal. From there the group went by train to Haifa where heavy equipment for the project was to be unloaded.

In 1917, the British Foreign Secretary had made the historic Balfour Declaration which recommended that a home should be made for the Jews in Palestine which was at that time under Turkish rule as part of the Ottoman Empire. It wasn't just altruism. Britain was seeking the support of European Jews for the Allied cause in the Great War, which was then still raging. After the war, Britain acquired a mandate over Palestine and was entrusted by the League of Nations to work out how to accommodate the national aspirations of both Jews and Arabs. But the Arabs were not prepared to accommodate the establishment of a Jewish state in Palestine. However, Hitler's persecution of the German Jews in the 30's led to numbers of them seeking to migrate to Palestine. Many were successful, but British authorities sought to limit the influx as Arab opposition to it grew. But after the end of the war in 1945, displaced Jews in great numbers, many of them concentration camp survivors, started arriving in Palestine. Every attempt was made to turn them back by British authorities. Cyprus became a detention centre for Jews caught trying to enter Palestine illegally. Nevertheless, the Jewish population of Palestine was increasing rapidly, and fighting between Arabs and Jews became commonplace with the British army and police struggling to control the situation.

When Richard arrived in Haifa, the situation was tense. Terrorist attacks were happening all the time. He soon found out that although it was reasonably safe to go out during the day, night time was a different story. If you were out and challenged to declare yourself you would be shot if the answer didn't suit, and if you rushed for cover, you would probably be shot anyway. When fighting flared up, the British would bring out their Staghounds, armoured cars, to quell the disturbance. But they were incapable of dealing with terrorist attacks such as the Arab slaughter of Jews working at the oil refinery, or the Jewish bombing of a police station. These incidents undermined British authority and moves to take stronger action only provoked retaliation. A classic example of this occurred when three Jewish terrorists were arrested for a raid on Acre prison releasing many of the prisoners, ironically, more Arabs than Jews. The terrorists were sentenced to death, in response to which the Jewish Irgun terrorist group captured two British sergeants and threatened to execute them if the death sentences on the Jews were carried out. They were. The following morning the sergeants were found hanging in a eucalyptus grove.

After several weeks in Haifa, Richard was glad to move to a base camp at Al Mafraq in northern Trans-Jordan where all the heavy equipment for constructing the pipeline was readied for operation. The equipment included rotary ditch diggers, back-loaders, tractors, low - loaders, fuel bowsers, lorries and jeeps. The operation then set up a tented camp at H3, a remote desert location in Western Iraq. It was a pumping station on the existing pipeline. The initial task was to excavate a deep trench running thirty miles to the west, and thirty miles to the east of H3. When that was completed, the operations camp would move sixty miles further along the planned route to do the same again. This procedure was to be repeated until the pipeline was finished.

Richard had six rotary diggers at his disposal and was keen to start training the local Arabs chosen to do the work. The method he employed was to train one operator on the first machine with another observing. When satisfied that the operator was competent, he assigned him to the second machine along with a new observer. He then trained the first observer to become a competent operator with a new observer watching. When satisfied with his performance, he allocated him the third machine along with a new observer. Continuing this, he trained twelve operators to use the rotary diggers. They learnt quickly as most of them already had driving skills acquired through working with British forces during the war. The pair assigned to each machine worked in shifts as it was dusty work and often almost unbearably hot. The operators were also trained in the maintenance of the machines, and on when and how to replace the teeth on their huge rotating drums.

The ground was sometimes too resistant for the rotary diggers. When hard rock was struck, the blasting team would be brought in. All were Arabs with a British supervisor. A ripper would be used to make some sort of trench, then the charges would be laid in it and fuses lit. It was dangerous work, and accidents happened, particularly if a charge didn't go off as expected and one of the workers went to investigate too soon. The blasts were so powerful that sometimes they would take down telephone poles and wires that ran along the route of the existing pipeline. Safety increased when the fuse method was replaced with an electrical detonation system where just one person operated the plunger when all were clear of the site. But it was never totally safe, even if the accidents merely involved mishandling of stolen detonators.

Once the operators were trained, Richard was told to move back into Palestine. It was expected that fighting between the Arabs and the Jews would only get worse as more Jewish immigrants arrived illegally. Consequently, it was thought that the best policy would be to complete the pipeline between Haifa and the Jordan River as soon as possible. He was booked into an Arab hotel in Nazareth, which was halfway along this section, and moved out daily in a small pick-up truck to supervise work at different sites. By going from Nazareth to Tiberias on the Sea of Galilee and then south to Jisr Mejamie, the river Jordan crossing, he and his Arab assistant and interpreter travelled to the eastern part of the Haifa - Jordan section mainly through Arab territory. It was safer than the direct route from Nazareth, but not completely so. The problem was one of identification. Was he Jew or Arab? Was he a spy for either? Was he working for the British authorities? Several times he had difficulty trying to convince armed sceptics of his true identity and of what he was doing in Palestine.

On one occasion near Tiberias, he was driving a lorry with a pick-up truck on the tray. He came to a halt because the lorry had developed a rattle and he wanted to check it out. There was some shooting taking place, but he had no reason to think that he was the target. But after he got out and started inspecting the lorry, bullets hit the ground around him. Firing was coming from an olive grove a short distance from the road. Then men emerged from it and advanced towards the vehicle. They were Arabs, and because Richard obviously wasn't, they were deeply suspicious of why he was in an Arab area. His limited Arabic didn't help, and when he called for assistance from his Arab companion, he got no help as his companion was petrified by the sight of the guns. If the Arabs decided Richard was a Jew, he knew he would be regarded as a collaborator, and that would mean only one thing! Fortunately they had time on their hands. Time to send for the headman of the village. He was educated and not so disposed to jump to conclusions as the others. Richard suggested that the headman accompanied him to Nazareth where his position could be proved by the authorities. Eventually, the headman was convinced he was who he said he was; a foreign worker on the pipeline. After that, Richard made a point of regularly stopping in that village and having a coffee and a chat with the headman and some of the other men. It was good insurance.

But he wasn't known in every Arab village between Nazareth and Tiberias. Once, when one of the tyres punctured on the low-loader he was driving, he found he couldn't change the wheel as the hydraulic jack had lost its oil. His Arab assistant said they could get oil in a nearby village, so they off-loaded the pick-up truck they had been carrying to get them there. When they arrived, Richard suggested that he stayed in the pick-up while his assistant went to get the oil. Richard was happy to put his head back and have a rest. But that was shortlived as some Arab children, spying the stranger in their midst, yelled repeatedly, "*Jehudi, Jehudi!*" The commotion brought men to the scene who dragged Richard from the pick-up and began marching him away, despite his protestations that he was not a Jew. Just as he was starting to fear the worst, his assistant arrived back on the scene in the company of another Arab who fortunately had previously worked with Richard. His cordial greeting defused the situation instantly. An Arab policeman even turned up, listened to what had happened, and made his release official.

"That was a close one," said Richard as they made their way back to the low - loader.

A few days later, on that same road, returning to Nazareth at the end of the day, he came across four British soldiers standing beside an army lorry. He pulled over and got out, suspecting they were in trouble. As soon as he spoke, they lowered their weapons. "Bloody

Geordie," said one of them. Their lorry had broken down and couldn't easily be fixed. He offered to take them to Nazareth or to their battalion headquarters at Tiberias. But they wouldn't leave the vehicle. They believed it would almost certainly be ransacked.

"O.K. then," said Richard, "I'll go back to Tiberias and tell them where you are and what's happened."

They thanked him for that, and he turned back towards the Sea of Galilee. It was dark when he got to the main gate of the battalion's headquarters. He attracted the attention of the sentry who told him to keep his distance. The sentry called an officer who listened to him as he shouted from a distance of thirty yards about the plight of the soldiers.

"They'll have to wait 'til morning," shouted the officer.

"Do you want me to tell them that?" responded Richard.

"If you're going back that way."

"If I can go back that way, why can't you lot?"

The officer thought about that, shuffling his feet, as if reluctant to reply. Then he did. "Ambush," he shouted, and dismissively waved Richard off.

As he drove back, he wasn't sure what was making him angry most, the thought that the officer was too cowardly to risk a night rescue of his men, or the thought that the officer might have even suspected Richard of luring him into an ambush. And that it was a northern England battalion as well. My accent should have been enough, he thought. He stopped to tell the soldiers that he had reported their situation, but that they might have to wait some time. But he didn't tell them what he really thought.

∗   ∗   ∗

Hopes that conditions would be peaceful enough for the Palestine end of the pipeline to be finished, proved to be wishful thinking. As conflict escalated, Richard and the trenching group were pulled out and deployed again on the Trans-Jordan and Iraq section. Richard was based back in a tented camp at H3. The repair workshops were there. Daily he would travel in a pick-up with an Arab assistant to locations where trenching was underway to check the equipment and make sure it was being maintained properly. If anything broke down, he would take the low-loader and bring it back to the workshops.

After twelve months he was appointed transport manager for the operation. Of the seventeen who had come out from England with him on the Queen Elizabeth to work on the project, only he and the chief engineer were left. Other replacements came, but like the others who had left, they couldn't take the heat and cold of the desert, and many resorted too much to drink. They didn't appreciate the beauty of the desert as Richard did. The blood red dawns and sunsets, the dust storms and the occasional downpours. And best of all, the majestic sight of the nomadic herders moving camp. Hundreds of camels in long lines, some with carriages perched on top in which the women were protected from the heat and dust, all casting long shadows in the morning sun.

The British Government became increasingly disenchanted with its mandate in Palestine as the situation between Jew and Arab went from bad to worse. In 1947 it turned to the United Nations to find an answer to the problem. A U.N. Committee of Study recommended an end to the British mandate and the setting up of a Jewish and an Arab state. A vote in the United Nations General Assembly endorsed this partition, despite Arab opposition to it. Terrorism escalated, and Jews even became targets in other parts of the Arab world. In May 1948, the mandate came to an end. The United States of America recognised the new state of Israel as did the Soviet Union. Egypt, the Trans-Jordanian Arab Legion, and the Arab Liberation Army invaded Israel from the south, east and north.

Richard left the project. He went by road to Beirut and flew home via Istanbul. He had been away twenty two months and had only had leave back to London once in that time. The pipeline was in limbo. The Americans who were responsible for the actual pipe work were withdrawn. The Arabs blamed the Americans for the setting up of Israel. The situation was too hostile for the project to proceed.

15

QATAR
1948

Richard was glad to be back home, well removed from the war raging in and around Israel. And Joan was glad to get help with the children who had now started school. Evelyn and Duncan were able to have time with their father, instead of having to explain to their teachers and school friends that daddy was in the desert where people rode around on camels. Joan, of course, never told them about the bullets and the bombs which he had mentioned in his letters.

After two months at home, he saw an advertisement in the newspaper for a job working for Scottish contractors in Qatar. It was similar to the one he'd had in Palestine, only this time building roads. He applied and got it. He flew out to Bahrein via Malta, and from Bahrein went by coastal steamer to Doha, the capital of Qatar. From there he travelled by road to Umm Said where an oil terminal was being constructed for the export of oil from wells in the west of the state. There was no trouble in Qatar, which was why Richard was prepared to go there, and why Joan was prepared to let him go. He had already used up his quota of nine lives in Spain and Palestine, and now with a family to worry about, he could do without the risks of war. Qatar was a British Protectorate and had been since the Great War. It was ruled by an Emir and the subjects were all of Islamic faith.

Umm Said, on the Persian Gulf, wasn't much of a place when he arrived. There was a small jetty for receiving equipment and food supplies, and a desalination plant for fresh water. Roads had to be constructed to connect the supply jetty and the oil terminal. The area was flat and flood prone, and the roads had to be built up to a metre above the surrounding plain. Work had already commenced on the roads but progress was slow. Richard told the agent for the Scottish company that if this was to change, he would have to be put in charge of the workmen, training them in the use of the equipment and supervising them, and for that to happen, the European supervisors already there would have to be shifted to other jobs. The agent agreed.

The heavy equipment available for the task included four huge tournapulls with rear-mounted scrapers, and a number of bulldozers, tractors and an old Bedford lorry with a crash gear box. There were also two draglines but they had Scottish operators who were not responsible to him. When the tournapulls arrived in crates they had to be assembled, and the Arab operators trained in their use and in the handling of the other equipment. His plan was to train two operators for each tournapull so that they could work shifts throughout the eight hour day. At first, he used the old Bedford lorry for training before he put them on the tournapulls. Some of the operators had done no more than ride a bicycle before they started the programme. They worked six days a week. Sunday was maintenance day, and some of the operators would stay back to help in the servicing of the vehicles. Others would go home to their families in Doha.

One of the problems was getting motors started in the morning. Richard would wake at dawn to find his tent covered in dew. Even his blanket. Opening the flap, he would be greeted by the familiar fog caused by moisture from the Persian Gulf condensing during the cold cloudless night. The vehicles were covered with tarpaulins to try to keep them dry. It helped a bit, but when it was really bad, it could be mid-morning before some vehicles were up and running. He found the Caterpillars the easiest to get going by using their petrol donkey engines before switching over to diesel. But the tournapulls, with direct battery start, had to be towed to get them going. Once running they were fine for the rest of the day. The operators became very skilled. The tournapull drivers thought of themselves as an elite. Locals used to come and watch them manoeuvering the giant machines.

At regular intervals everything stopped while all the workers prayed to Allah. Richard found this strange. It hadn't happened in Iraq. There they just used to pray in the breaks. However, he didn't try to stop the practice. The company rule was to respect the local culture. They were proud people and expected to be treated with dignity. That expectation led to an incident which involved the local sheik. One of the Sunday maintenance jobs involved servicing the winches. Sand and dust used to get into them, and the bearings had to be taken out, cleaned and greased. One of the Arab workmen accidently dropped a just-greased bearing into the sand. In annoyance, Richard, without thinking, pushed him. His dignity had been affronted. He claimed assault and reported the incident. A sheik came down from Doha to hear the case in a specially set up marquee. Richard half-expected to be on the next flight home. But he wasn't even called to give his side of the story. Instead, he was required to make an apology. Face was saved, dignity restored.

Using such heavy equipment, there was always the possibility of accident and injury. Sometimes a tournapull lurched off the 'highway' and pulling it back up took a lot of time and effort. The only serious injury was when an Arab workman, standing too close to the side of a working tournapull, got his robe caught in the deep tread of the tyre. He suffered severe friction burns before the vehicle was stopped. He was rushed to the first-aid post from where he was transferred to hospital in Doha. Later he returned to Umm Said on light duties, helping to service the vehicles.

Richard was at Umm Said for twelve months. The first tanker came in before he left. Its crew was from the Scottish Highlands. They were welcomed ashore to celebrate the opening of the terminal, and he enjoyed mixing again with merchant navy types. He had a lot in common with them.

When the road-building was finished, he was transferred to the tractor workshops at Doha, organizing the repair work. He liked the work and the responsibility and also the local beach. A special bonus was that the food provided by the company was excellent. He wanted Joan to come out and live there. The children could have gone to the English school in Bahrein, and she could have picked up nursing work in Bahrein or Doha. But she thought otherwise. And when he returned to England on leave with a huge blister on his nose, she did her best to persuade him to come home. He had got the blister in an accident outside the workshops. A road tanker went on fire as a result of a welding spark. The fire was in the oil tank itself which was belching flames and thick smoke from out of the top opening. Richard started up a bulldozer with a view to piling up earth to isolate the tanker from the rest of the workshops. He was handed gloves and a welding mask for protection from the heat. Unfortunately, his nose was in contact with the front of the mask.

On his return from leave, he just couldn't settle back into the job. Not only did Joan want him back home, but Evelyn and Duncan wanted their dad as well. He resigned.

16

SUDAN
1951

When Richard flew into London he thought he was home for good. The children were growing up quickly. Joan had regular nursing work and after all his long absences in the Middle East, there was a lot of catching up to do. They weren't poor. The overseas jobs paid well and almost all his living costs had been met by the company. The food had usually been good although the accommodation had often been in tents, especially in Iraq. Most of the money he earned he had sent home for Joan to use or bank. He hadn't needed much. He didn't drink. Not seriously. He didn't smoke. It was his nature to be thrifty. Consequently he started looking for work not long after he got back. Jack Olding's, the Caterpillar company, offered him work again doing repairs in the workshop. He was glad of that. But it was early 1951. Britain was still recovering from the war, wages were low and rationing was still in place. Even the children had to hand over sweet coupons with their pennies to buy their liquorice allsorts. Life wasn't easy

After nine months of domesticity, a position as mechanical superin-tendent came up with the Government of Sudan. It involved train-ing locals to use and maintain road-building equipment. Again the money was attractive and would help to pay for Evelyn and

Duncan's private school fees. The children had now established a good relationship with their father, which had been a concern of Joan's during his time in the Middle East, and as the Sudan was not thought of as a trouble spot, Joan let him apply. He was interviewed and got the position, almost certainly on the strength of his previous experience, and particularly because of his demonstrable staying power. He didn't quit when the going got tough.

The Sudan was not completely free of trouble. It was under Anglo-Egyptian control, but there was a strong independence movement. This, however, was split between the Umma group which wanted independence from both Britain and Egypt, and the Ashigga group which, while wanting independence from Britain, wanted union with Egypt. A further source of tension in Sudan was between the Arab majority of Islamic faith in the north and the Negro minority in the south, many of whom were Christian. The Negroes were distrustful of the Arabs, never forgetting that in the past, the Arabs had invaded the south seeking slaves. When Richard arrived in Khartoum in October 1951, he knew nothing of these political and social divisions, but was to learn about them as time passed

His first task was to run the training programme at the School of Instruction at Gordon's Tree on the outskirts of Khartoum. The school didn't actually exist on his arrival, but a site on empty land had been ear-marked for it. The school was quickly established by the Clerk of Works and Richard was provided with four instructors and two mechanics. The school was entirely under canvas, and included a workshop and classroom, a kitchen and mess and accommodation. The machines on which the trainees practised were new, specially purchased for the school. They included graders, bulldozers,tournapulls, front-end loaders, low-loaders and tip-trucks. The course lasted six weeks and was of a very intensive nature with only ten trainees on each course. It had to be as most of them had never driven vehicles of any type before. Nevertheless, he found them enthusiastic and capable. Once moderately competent, the trainees practised their skills constructing a new Khartoum airfield and also a number of fish ponds. If some were not sufficiently skilled at the end of six weeks, government authorities would insist that rather than failing them, the course be extended for them so that they could come up to the required standard. On completion of the course, each operator was tested and given certificates stating which items of equipment he was qualified to use. One hundred operators had graduated from the school by the time he was assigned to another position.

When Richard left Gordon's Tree, the school was closed. It had done its job. Now there was a group of skilled operators of earth-moving equipment available for construction projects in any part of Sudan. He had enjoyed the work and only one serious accident marred the school's record, and that wasn't his fault. He had heard from inside the workshop a sudden commotion. He rushed outside to find a group milling round the end of a stationary low-loader which was carrying a front-end loader. When he got through the throng, there was a young Sudanese boy with his leg smashed by the front-end loader's jib arm. He jumped into the cabin, raised the arm off the boy and called one of the European instructors to take him to hospital straight away. The instructor took one look at the injury and nearly fainted. He had to do the job himself. He knew well what had happened. When he had rushed out at the sound of the commotion, he had noticed one of the local fitters in the cabin of the front-end loader. He had obviously been playing with the controls and released the jib arm. It was the boy's bad luck to have been sitting on the back of the low-loader. His leg was amputated. Richard visited him in hospital several times taking him fruit and sweets, and when he had been fitted with an artificial leg, he returned to the camp and Richard found odd jobs for him to do. There was an inquiry into the incident, but it was deemed to be just an unfortunate accident. No one was charged.

Richard's next assignment was to Suakin, a port on the Red Sea. Roads were being constructed in the area and his job was to supervise the servicing and repairs of the machinery in the workshops. A number of European fitters were employed there. He and his Sudanese co-driver left Khartoum with a lorry load of spares. Close to Suakin, they passed a British army camp and were impressed to see regimental insignias carved out of the cliff face overlooking the camp. Brilliantly painted, they lit up in the setting sun, each one proclaiming its territory. After two months supervising the workshops and construction sites, he returned to Khartoum and reported to the Government authorities that all was in order at Suakin.

While in Khartoum, Richard saw the first signs of political unrest. A group demanding an independent Sudan infiltrated the city, weapons hidden beneath their robes. They surrounded the Governor's Palace. It was a good time to take leave. A month later, he returned and was sent to Al - Ubayyid, a town two hundred miles south west of Khartoum where road building was taking place. It was back to life in a tent, doing the same job as the one at Suakin. He stayed there for eight months. Living in the desert had never been a problem for him. He had his own tent which was very roomy with two centre poles and four foot walls. It was equipped with a camp bed, folding table, a canvas hand basin on a stand and even a canvas bath. It was dusty work much of the time, yet a bath was still a luxury rather than a necessity given that water was scarce. But a personal water filter was a necessity. Richard's consisted of a stainless steel container with two chambers separated by a sandstone filter. It converted muddy water into clear water. But, of course, it didn't kill bacteria. Dysentery was common but he escaped it. His immune system worked well, but he drank mostly boiled water, as tea or coffee. His primus stove was to him an indispensable piece of equipment.

Richard's last posting in the Sudan was to Al Fashir in the far west. It was desert country which experienced unpredictable summer downpours. He was relieving a supervisor who had been in the west for many months. Again he wasn't starting a project. Road building and the construction of dams to trap the short-lived run-off from the summer downpours were taking place already. But there were always new sites to work on and new camps to establish. He arrived at Al Fashir with additional heavy equipment, including tournapulls and spare parts. He set up his personal tent and a workshop marquee on the outskirts of the town. From there he visited various construction sites, sometimes staying overnight and sleeping out in the open. He never feared for his own safety. He always treated the Sudanese with respect and got the same in return, but he did fear for the safety of the operators and if he saw any carelessness he would intervene. His well-honed personal survival skills enabled him to see an accident waiting to happen. Psychologists call it projection.

The security of his personal belongings was never a problem. When he left the base camp his tent was never interfered with. But there was one exception. One day, women from the local brickworks made signs indicating that they wanted him to give them a drink of water. It was hot and dusty and they were covered in perspiration. He nodded and went into his tent and brought out a mug and jug of water with ice cubes floating on the top. They were astonished to see ice cubes, and even more astonished when Richard popped one in his mouth. He brought out more for them, enjoying their excitement at the novelty. He shouldn't have done that. When he was away, some of the bolder women helped themselves out of his paraffin refrigerator. He had encouraged them, so he could only blame himself. And he didn't really mind as they touched nothing else.

Although Al Fashir was an isolated place, Richard didn't feel any great sense of isolation. Not only did he get along well with local Sudanese, he also became friendly with some of the other British in the town. One day the Governor's wife came to his tent on horseback with an invitation to dinner at the Residence. After that he was invited back there two or three times, but their hospitality was not reciprocated even though his tent was always spic and span. It just wasn't set up for hospitality. Many a meal was shared on work sites with the civil engineer, and he became very friendly with the Scottish doctor and his wife. One weekend he drove them in a government lorry to visit friends of theirs in the hill country well to the west of Al Fashir. The rugged desert scenery and the company of new friends made it a memorable day, but what made it even more memorable was that on the way back they were stopped and ordered to transport a young couple under arrest back to town. They both had their hands tied behind them and were placed under guard in the back of the lorry. The pair had eloped despite the girl being promised. When they reached town, the guard took them out of the back, and before Richard had time to drive off, a group of people had started stoning them.

"We can't interfere," said the doctor, responding to his wife's distress. "It's their law and they know the price."

*   *   *

Revolution in Egypt in 1952 had seen the Crown replaced by a Republic. After that, Sudan moved inexorably towards becoming a republic in its own right. The British presence became increasingly uneasy in the changing political climate. Now, a task which Richard had always disliked, that of recommending Sudanese operators for promotion, became even more uncomfortable. Joan wanted him home. Evelyn and Duncan were now teenagers. Despite being offered a further contract, he flew out of Khartoum for London in October 1955 with two months pay in his pocket. Good pay at that.

17

ADELAIDE, AUSTRALIA
1956

When Richard flew into London from the Sudan, winter was approaching. Although the home Joan had made in Welwyn Garden City was better set up and more comfortable than anything he'd ever known, he found it hard to settle back into suburban life. He found the smog, London's cold smoke-laden fog, generated by countless coal fires, hard to take after the heat and blue skies of Sudan. Evelyn and Duncan were still at school and Joan was working as a nurse in a medical practice. She got on well with Doctor Gilbert but when he told her that he was planning to migrate to New Zealand, it raised in her mind the idea that perhaps migration was an option for them. Richard's brother Cecil had migrated to New Zealand as a young lad. Surely Richard wouldn't be averse to moving to that part of the world, she thought. And then there's Australia. After all, he said he liked the friendliness of the Australians he had met when he went ashore there. But that was more than twenty years ago, she mused, but they would still be the same. She remembered those two Australian nurses at Colmenar that he couldn't praise enough in that Madrid broadcast he made.

Australia was seeking migrants from Britain at this time. The bombing of Darwin by the Japanese in the Second World War had created a sense of alarm among Australians about the ease with which the country could be invaded. In 1945 it only had a population of seven million. The Cold War and the perceived threat of communism fed this fear. The Australian government responded to the situation with inducements for Europeans, including refugees, to migrate and work in nation-building projects like the Snowy Mountains scheme. Britons were understandably favoured as migrants. Assisted passages, at first only by sea, were introduced. An adult could go to Australia for ten pounds. An entire family for twenty. There was a great deal of publicity in Britain about the scheme and how to apply for an assisted passage.

At this time Richard was working as a welder for a small contractor but it was a bit of a come-down after the responsibilities he'd had abroad. Joan wanted him home now that the children were teenagers but suspected that if he saw a good position with good money overseas, he would be sorely tempted. Migration would mean that they would all be going overseas with him. The family talked it over. Following a visit to Australia House where they watched a film showing the developments taking place in the country, they believed that they could settle in quickly once they arrived. Part of the film promoted the new satellite town of Elizabeth which was just north of the city of Adelaide in South Australia. It emphasised its Mediterranean climate and new housing, luxurious by ordinary British standards. They went round to South Australia House, where they were interviewed for assisted passages and were promptly accepted. With their savings added to the money they could expect to get from the sale of their Welwyn Garden City house, they had more than enough to buy a new house at Elizabeth. They also had enough to buy a car, a Vauxhall, to take out with them. As ten pound Poms they would be well set up.

*　　*　　*

The atmosphere on the migrant ship, the Otranto, that left Southampton in June had a special chemistry. A mix of emotions. Feelings of regret for having left relatives and friends behind who might never be seen again, apprehension about what lay ahead and the excitement and novelty of adventure. Richard and Joan and family were probably more relaxed than many of the other passengers. They had the money to set up a new home and the car, which they had been able to use right up to the last moment in England, would arrive on another ship not long after their own arrival. And Richard had already been there twenty five years before, in the Dalblair. He was one up on the others. The Mediterranean, the Suez Canal and the Red Sea were all familiar to him.

"This is where I got the train to Haifa," he said at Ismailia. "That's when I went to work on the pipe line."

"We off-loaded coal from Mombasa somewhere over there," he said, pointing to the hazy coast of Saudi Arabia.

Life on board was crowded but the discomforts bearable. There was entertainment, particularly dancing at night, and the usual ceremony of crossing the Equator. Despite the blandness of the food, the air of expectation kept everyone's spirits up, and who could complain when it was costing next to nothing.

*　　*　　*

It was late July when the ship berthed at Outer Harbour, Port Adelaide, and after going through Customs and Migration, the family caught the train into Adelaide along with many other families. It was only the shortest of walks from the Adelaide railway station on

North Terrace to the Elder Park hostel. Richard and Joan were given a small room with twin beds separated by a narrow walkway. "It's like being back in Spain," joked Richard.

"How do you mean?" responded a puzzled Joan.

"Well, it's like being in the back of the ambulance again." They both laughed at the thought.

"Anyway," he added, "We're better off than Evelyn and Duncan. At least we're not in dormitories and we do have our privacy."

Although it was mid-winter in Adelaide, they all woke up to find the sun shining brightly and not a cloud in the sky. They could barely wait to look around, but Joan insisted that they all got breakfast first in the cafeteria. The hostel's location, being just behind the Adelaide railway station, meant that they simply had to cross North Terrace and they were in the city centre. King William Street, the main thoroughfare, was less than a hundred yards away, and Rundle Street, the shopping centre, was also very close as it led off from King William Street. When they got to Rundle Street it was teeming with people going to work, waving to or smiling at friends as they went in through different doors. Others, mostly young women smartly dressed in the uniforms of the shops and stores, were chatting in an animated fashion, trying to get their messages finished before they too dashed inside. In the bright winter sunshine, the bustle of the street contrasted with the blue-green stillness of the Mount Lofty Ranges which seemed to loom over its eastern end. It was hard to take it all in after the dourness of the London they had left behind.

"It seems so alive," said Richard, to anyone listening. Enjoying the sun on his face, he shaded his eyes and pointed to the Ranges.

"Look at that!" he said slowly and with emphasis. "They're gum trees, eucalypts. Wait till you smell them." Then, turning to Joan, he said, "You know, I haven't felt so good for a long time. We've done the right thing."

"Reminds me of Spain," replied Joan. "I think it's the clarity. I feel as if I could reach out and almost touch those hills."

*   *   *

The first thing they wanted to do was to check up on the house they intended to buy in Elizabeth. They were told at the hostel to contact the Housing Trust. It was arranged for them to be picked up to be taken for a look around Elizabeth, to choose either a vacant block or a house. The car came for them and the driver introduced himself as Mr. Ramsay. It was his own car, he said, and on the journey he explained that he was the manager of the Housing Trust and that he welcomed the opportunity to take them round as it helped him check up on the progress of the development. He enjoyed discussing with Richard and Joan the pros and cons of the different locations. He responded to any questions in an open and friendly manner. They settled on a house already started on Harvey Road, facing on to a reserve and with a view of the hills. At the time the walls were up but not the roof. They expected it to be completed soon, but it took eight months to be finished as the Housing Trust was running low on funds. They were offered other completed houses, but they had set their minds on Harvey Road.

They just had to put up with the delay over the house, and life in the hostel had one big advantage. Being right in the city meant it was easier to look for work. Evelyn soon got a job as a typist and Duncan got work at Healing's on King William Street. It was a business which sold a wide range of goods, from refrigerators to car parts. Joan found a position as a part-time cashier at Balfour's, a major city bakery.Richard was hoping to get work close to Elizabeth so that he wouldn't have far to travel, but there was not much available. The Holden car plant didn't open up there until 1962, and in 1956 there were quite a number of unemployed people in Elizabeth. He didn't like being unemployed, particularly when the rest of the family had jobs. He was attracted by a place as a mechanic on a sheep station on the Nullarbor Plain. He was accepted after an interview in the company's King William Street office, but Joan ruled that out even though the whole family could have lived there. Another one that Joan ruled out was working for the Highways' Department at Port Lincoln. He would have been in charge of the heavy equipment. "Just down my street," he said. "That's a street too far!" was Joan's reply. "Elizabeth it is!" Then, like manna from heaven, Richard saw an advertisement in South Australia's morning newspaper, aptly called The Advertiser, for positions at the Weapons Research Establishment at Salisbury. W.R.E., as it was locally known, was only a short distance from Elizabeth. The position was for a mechanic in the diesel workshop. He applied and was interviewed, then called in for a second interview. Although he knew that his experience with tanks and earthmoving equipment stood him in good stead, he was on tenterhooks when he fronted up for the second interview. He expected them to raise the part he played in the Spanish Civil War, and to ask him bluntly, if he was or ever had been a member of the Communist Party. But they didn't and he got the job. He would never know if they knew about his past. Later, he would come to believe that they didn't, as at that time anti-communism was rife because of the Cold War.

Richard thoroughly enjoyed the commitment to excellence which pervaded the diesel workshop. The main work was servicing diesel generators which were used to provide electricity in remote locations, such as the Giles Weather Station, and in and around Woomera and Maralinga. The equipment had to be sent out in perfect working order, as breakdowns in the outback could disrupt weapons testing programmes.

18

GIBSON DESERT AND ANNA PLAINS

In 1958 there was a call in the diesel workshop for a volunteer mechanic to take part in a mapping expedition in central Australia. Richard volunteered and was chosen. The job involved looking after all the vehicles, driving one of them and being chief cook.

The expedition started with three vehicles leaving Adelaide loaded with supplies, most from W.R.E. sources. Woomera Rocket Range Reconnaissance Officer, Trevor Nossiter, was expedition leader. He and a W.R.E. colleague, who was not to stay with the expedition, were driving Landrovers and Richard, with the biggest share of equipment and supplies was driving a Unimog, a coil springed high clearance diesel, selected because of its ability to cope with sandy terrain. Where the others might get bogged, it wouldn't. The Unimog had two characteristics which caused him much frustration. Its speed was governed to thirty miles per hour, which meant he was invariably trailing behind. Of course they would stop from time to time to allow him to catch up, then they would set off again as soon as he did. They got periodic rests, he didn't. The other characteristic was that because of its springing, every bump on the road caused it to rock like a small boat in a rough sea.

At Port Augusta, they joined the Stuart Highway, travelling past Woomera and Coober Pedy. At a pre-arranged point, they were joined by Beadell, a skilled surveyor and bushman; McDougall, an expert in Aboriginal languages, and a third man who was a cartographer. The spare driver left the party leaving five of them, each with his own vehicle.

The mapping exercise really started from Giles Weather Station. The objective was to map a route for a road across the Gibson Desert to Marble Bar and Port Hedland. Beadell and the cartographer selected the route and Richard followed in the rear. In the evenings, Richard would pitch camp and prepare a hot meal, with Beadell offering unsolicited advice. At first Beadell hadn't realised Richard knew as much about deserts as himself. Conversation around the campfires was always convivial as all of them had many stories to tell. The cartographer would probably have won first prize if there had been one. He had met the infamous Sundown murderer who was tried and hung in Adelaide for shooting three station people in the Alice Springs area. At the time, he explained, he had been on a caravan holiday with his wife and daughter. They were in the Northern Territory-South Australia border area, and had just passed through a gate on the road when a black car towing a small caravan came the other way. He did the courteous thing and held the gate open for them so they wouldn't have to stop. It was a man and woman in the car. He thought they looked a bit strange, not as friendly as people almost always are in the bush, particularly when done a favour. He closed the gate after them and thought no more about it until he heard on the news about the murders over the car radio, along with a request for anyone to come forward for questioning who had even just been in the area of the crime. He went to the police and told them about the couple. They were arrested in Mt Isa. He believed the fellow's wife had told the police what had happened, and he forever thanked his lucky stars that he and his wife and daughter hadn't become victims themselves.

Well, even Beadell couldn't cap that one, but he did have some humorous tales to tell. Also he could give a fine show with a stock whip which he did for them at the first cattle station they came to out of the Gibson. He also had something of a reputation as a medic, and would pull teeth if requested, a service which remote Aborigines appreciated. After several days of bumping through the bush, Richard thought he would avail himself of that service. He had a terrible toothache from the jarring, but insisted that Beadell gave him an injection first to kill the pain. But it didn't work, nor did the second injection. Richard lost faith in him and refused the bush dentistry. After they got on to better roads at Marble Bar, the pain had disappeared.

Throughout the journey in the Gibson Desert they saw very little wildlife except for lizards. But they did see plenty of animal scats and camel footprints. The sounds of five vehicles crashing through the spinifex would have been so alien to wildlife that they must have scattered long before any vehicles got near them. They didn't see any Aborigines either. McDougall didn't have the opportunity to use his language skills.

Once they had reached cattle country, Richard and Nossiter went on to Marble Bar and Port Hedland, and from there drove north along the coastal road to Anna Plains station. The others, their duties finished for the time being, went elsewhere. At Anna Plains they made contact with the station owner who already knew of their purpose.

That was to set up a base camp close to the impact zone for the British Blue Streak rocket tests. The area would have to be explored carefully before the site for the base camp was determined. There wasn't time for that to be carried out just then. Nossiter had to get back to W.R.E.. They left the Unimog at the station, returned to Port Hedland and flew back to Adelaide's R.A.A.F. Edinburgh air base at Salisbury.

After a short period back in the diesel workshop, Nossiter called on Richard to accompany him on a return visit to Anna Plains, this time with the purpose of deciding where to establish a base camp. They flew to Port Hedland and from there went by road to Anna Plains. They pitched their camp only a short drive away from the station homestead.

The coastal area was flat with little relief. Vegetation was sparse, consisting mostly of bunch grasses and scattered trees. Inland lay the Great Sandy Desert where a succession of dunes, often steep at their crests, stretched into the distance. And spinifex everywhere.

They scouted the area over several days in search of alternative base camp sites. However, once inland, travel in the sand-dune country was difficult. Nossiter decided that where they had pitched camp initially was as good a site as any as it could be accessed readily by road from Port Hedland through which most construction materials, personnel and supplies would come. Also it was suitable for the establishment of an airfield. So they set up the beginnings of Talgarno which was intended to be a miniature Woomera set in its own 'prohibited area', an area stretching south from Broome almost to Port Hedland and two hundred miles inland into the desert. The preliminary camp at Talgarno was equipped with a short-wave radio and a Flying Doctor Service radio, both housed in a high

218

security locked hut. Power and lighting were provided by diesel generators to the radio hut, to a small wooden mess hut, and to the tented accommodation. All communication on the short wave radio had to be logged. Regular contact was made with Woomera and W.R.E.Adelaide. The Flying Doctor Service radio was not simply used for medical emergencies. It was the local news service for the stations, a sharing of information from important events to gossip. Richard flew back to W.R.E. with Nossiter and went back to Anna Plains with him several times to check out equipment until finally he was put permanently in charge of site maintenance. At this stage major construction had not commenced and Talgarno had only four personnel, a Commonwealth security officer, a cook and a mechanic to assist Richard. Typical of the times, the security officer saw Reds under the beds, his suspicions enhanced by frequent bouts with the bottle. Once he was convinced he could see the lights of a Russian submarine offshore, and it took Richard some time to shake that conviction.

"I tell you, it's the evening star! I spent years at sea. I should know. It's the evening star!"

The security officer even interrogated a road gang working nearby, suspecting it might be providing cover for a communist spy. The puzzled foreman afterwards asked Richard, "What's he on about? Spies out here! There's bugger all to spy on." It was a good job the officer didn't know about Richard's time in Spain and in the Party. He kept quiet about that.

Supplies for Talgarno were obtained mainly from Port Hedland, but sometimes from Broome. The site was visited from time to time by government people, ministers and public servants, and a large wooden mess was built to provide for them. Townley, the Minister for Supply, used to stay at the Anna Plains homestead, particularly if he was on his own or just with one other. But usually visitors stayed in Port Hedland, at one of the two hotels which faced each other on either side of the main street. Port Hedland was a rough place in the fifties with many more men than women in the town. This was well reflected in the clientele of the pub, both the boarders and the drinkers, not that the boarders didn't drink. Once when a large party of government people, Commonwealth and State, came to Talgarno, Nossiter had to use both hotels in Port Hedland for accommodation. At one of them, the landlord indicated that he would put them up in rooms which happened to be vacant, mixing them with the common herd. Nossiter tried to see if his guests could be allocated adjacent rooms in a reserved section of the hotel, seeing that they were very important people. V.I.P's, he called them. "I couldn't give a bugger who they are," was the landlord's response. And the next morning he demonstrated this by waking them up to his rhythmic pounding on a pogo stick on the hotel verandah. He was clad only in vest and shorts. The civilities of Canberra, Adelaide and Perth were alien to Port Hedland!

"I think the pollies learnt a few new words as well," commented Richard, as he and Nossiter discussed what had happened.

"You don't know politicians."

$$* \quad * \quad *$$

Interesting characters used to come to Anna Plains from time to time. Two brothers who were water borers came and camped nearby for a week or so, and Richard became friendly with them. They had lots of stories to tell. Then on a trip to Port Hedland for supplies, he was astonished to come across a cyclist travelling north. He stopped and they exchanged a few words. Then, when he got back, he found the fellow camped with the borers. He did some work for them in exchange for supplies, then went on his way. Some travellers became a nuisance as they used to regard homesteads as general stores where they could get supplies of fuel, water, tinned food, flour and the like. They would help themselves to tank water and sometimes leave gates open. But most showed respect for property. Sometimes Richard went to Broome for supplies. It was like a foreign place with Malay pearling luggers lying at anchor and shops run by Chinese. Once he went with Nossiter and they stayed overnight at the hotel. The landlord showed them his pearl collection which must have been worth a small fortune. On the same trip they called in at the Lagrange Mission which was run by a Catholic order, the Pallotine Fathers. They were treated to a pleasant meal. Many Aboriginal children were cared for at the mission, and numbers of adults were camped in the area around it. From what he saw there, Richard formed the view that the adult males seemed to have nothing to do. Perhaps because they were not able to get work as stockmen. His observations gave birth to what he thought was a great idea. If Talgarno was to become a small town, there would be a demand for construction workers. Having trained Arabs with no previous skills how to use earthmoving equipment he believed he could train Aborigines just as easily. He presented his proposal to Nossiter and it was given serious consideration higher up, possibly because someone in authority saw it as an interesting experiment. But nothing happened for sometime. Then, out of the ether, courtesy of the Flying Doctor Service radio, it was announced that Aborigines were to be trained as construction workers for the building of Talgarno, and once trained, were to be given award wages. Every station which employed Aboriginal stockmen for nominal wages and their keep was, to say the least, stunned by such news.

With that approval, he went to Lagrange with a view to discussing with the Mission fathers the recruiting of Aborigines. He expected them to be enthusiastic but they were just the opposite. Uncooperative, as if to say, we don't want anyone taking our black-fellas.

*   *   *

Woody Pearce, the station owner at Anna Plains, had become very friendly with Richard long before the Aboriginal training proposal. At times when there was not much to do on site, he would volunteer to help Woody around the station. Woody was pleased to have both the company and the help. The drought was on and it was necessary to go around the property regularly to check that the cattle had at least water even if there wasn't much feed. The wind pumps had to be checked and the troughs cleaned up. As the drought continued and the area around the troughs became eaten out, the stock had to move an ever increasing distance between feed and water. This weakened them so much that when the very weakest got back to a trough, they would sometimes collapse across it. Others would drink so much that when they tried to move off, they fell over and just didn't have the strength to get up again. If they were still alive when found, Woody would put them out of their misery with his 303. Richard had asked Woody what the chains were for in the back of the Landrover. "You'll see," he said, and he soon did. They were for dragging away cattle which had died around the troughs.

"Only the fittest cattle survive when it gets really bad," said Woody. "It's called natural selection."

Once while Richard was at Anna Plains, there was a big round-up. A number of stockmen were involved, mostly blacks. The foreman was a one-armed white fellow, but he handled a horse well enough. Richard only watched. The occasional older bull, as if sensing it was being driven towards the pens, would break loose and race into the scrub. They were left to make good their escape. It would have taken more time and effort than it was worth to recover them. After the round-up, stock from Anna Plains was trucked south. Anna Plains was really just for breeding. Woody had other property down south, nearer Perth, which he used for fattening the cattle before sending them to the sale yards.

Woody wasn't just friendly with Richard. He and his wife invited all four at Talgarno to dinner at the homestead from time to time. Usually there would be one or two rouseabouts being fed there. They would eat on the verandah if they had a barbeque, but Mrs. Pearce was a good cook and could produce a variety of meals. If the weather was cool, they would be invited inside to have the meal around the huge kitchen table.

The Aboriginal stockmen were housed with their wives and families in quarters close to the homestead. The stockmen were indispensible to the running of the station. The Pearces treated them well by the standards of the time, providing them with their supplies and necessities. Of course, the stockmen were cheap labour. Richard thought that the Aboriginal men were better off there than at the Mission. At least they were properly employed.

Relations between the Pearces and the four at Talgarno became so friendly that once when Woody was away in Perth, Mrs. Pearce invited them to dinner. The occasion was due to the Aboriginal stockmen having presented Mrs. Pearce with a small shark which they had caught in a tidal trap. It was quite a feast and a welcome change from the usual fare. The four of them left the homestead about 10:30 at night, after thanking Mrs. Pearce for her hospitality. Richard went straight to bed and when he got up the next day, after breakfast and attending to one or two tasks, he decided to go back up to the homestead to thank Mrs. Pearce again for her hospitality the night before. When he got to the gate, the one-armed foreman came forward and told him he wasn't allowed in.

"Not until Mr. Pearce returns," he said.

Richard was dumbfounded. "What's all this about?" he asked. "I want to see Mrs. Pearce."

He must have raised his voice, because she came out onto the verandah and shouted, "You wait till Mr. Pearce comes back, he'll sort things out."

"What is there to sort out?"

"Well after you left last night, there was a commotion in the Aboriginal quarters. It could only have been you lot."

"Right, I'll find out about that," he replied indignantly, "and I'll let you know." With that, he hurried to the Landrover and sped back to the camp. The security officer had left and the mechanic wasn't in sight. He asked the cook if he knew anything about the incident in the Aboriginal quarters. He didn't, but said that some time after they had got back to camp, the security man and the mechanic had left the camp in a vehicle. He had heard them muttering something and then heard the sound of the vehicle driving off. Then he went back to sleep.

Richard returned to the homestead and managed to convey that much to Mrs. Pearce. He was still smarting at being thought guilty. Mrs. Pearce had contacted Woody about the incident already and had told him she thought that all four of them were involved. Woody had told his wife that he would take the matter to higher authority, and that he was coming back to the station straight away.

Concerned about his reputation and position, Richard wrote a letter to Nossiter outlining what had happened and drove into Port Hedland to post it. As soon as Woody got back, he came straight over to the camp not giving his wife the opportunity of changing her version of what had happened. Woody fiercely berated Richard for his part in the incident. When he had calmed down to the point where he was prepared to listen, Richard told him what he knew and that he had written to Nossiter stating exactly the same about what had happened. Woody now accepted his version of events. Then, over the short wave radio came news that a group was coming to Anna Plains to investigate the incident. Two days later, the group, consisting only of Nossiter and a senior security officer from Melbourne arrived in a R.A.A.F. plane which landed at the Anna Plains airstrip. By this time the local security officer was back at the camp. The inquiry was held in the radio hut. The two of them interviewed Woody and the local security officer together. Richard was waiting his turn but they didn't call him. Nossiter had his letter, of course. The inquiry didn't last long and Nossiter asked Richard to drive the senior officer back to the plane without being given any indications of of their findings. On the way, to add insult to injury, the senior officer started making excuses for the local officer's indiscretion. He was lonely, he said. And just as Richard was about to speak his mind, they arrived at the aircraft. The pilot came over to the vehicle and poked his head through the window. He had lost his chance to say his piece.

Two days later, Richard was recalled to Adelaide, not over the secure short wave radio but over the Flying Doctor service network. All the station people knew of his recall, in the same way as they all had heard about the incident itself. He was mortified. Now everyone would think he was the guilty party. Before he left, Woody invited him back up to the homestead. "No thanks, I think you've done enough," was his curt reply.

19

MARALINGA

Back in the diesel workshop at Salisbury, Richard was still fuming about what had happened and the way he was sent back from Anna Plains. He felt he had been dismissed. What made it worse was that it was all bottled up. Because of the high security surrounding the Blue Streak Project, he could not talk to any of his colleagues about what had happened, and could not even share his burden with Joan. He did talk to Nossiter, however, to tell him that he felt he had been badly treated. That didn't do him much good. Nossiter said there was nothing personal in it, there was no black mark against his name and he should just get on with the job. He had little choice short of resigning and he wouldn't do that, he enjoyed the work.

Nossiter was right about one thing. No black mark. A few months later, early in 1961, there was a call for a volunteer from the work-shop to go to Maralinga to be in charge of maintenance of its diesel generators. Richard volunteered and got the position.

The journey to Maralinga was a real treat. The Adelaide to Perth train took him almost all the way, and he had his own sleeping compartment. The Mount Lofty Ranges, east of Adelaide, extending north to become the rugged Flinders Ranges, were always in view as the train plodded north to Port Augusta. After that, it was desert scenery all the way to Watson on the Nullarbor Plain. Richard revelled in the sense of freedom which his return to the Australian outback gave him. He pondered on why he had come to love open spaces, wilderness, which many would regard as inhospitable wastelands. Was it because he was cooped up in that reform school for five years? Was it born of his fondness for the Pennine moorlands of northern England which provided release from the claustrophobic back streets of its industrial towns, or was it his feeling for the Spanish Meseta which he had criss-crossed with Joan in the ambulance? Perhaps it was his years in remote construction camps in Iraq, Qatar and Sudan. He wondered what the relatives and friends he knew in England would think about the landscape he was passing through. It would probably be raining there, he thought. They would be huddled around the range, popping another piece of coal on the fire, waiting for the kettle to boil for yet another cup of tea. He smiled to himself. They're still into cups of tea out here but without the milk. Aunt Ethel wouldn't like that!

At Watson he was picked up by a lorry and taken to Maralinga which was about fifty miles north of the railway. He was allocated a bed in ordinary quarters and taken to the mess for a meal. The food was top quality and plenty of it. That's a good start, he thought.

He soon realised that in a sense he was no longer working for the W.R.E. This was a British show and he was responsible to what was called the British Technical Department. Nevertheless, the mechanic who was to assist him was from the Australian Army's Royal Engineers. He helped with the greasing and servicing of the generators. Apart from looking after the generators, the job entailed moving them from test site to test site. The entire area was restricted and some areas within it highly restricted with many signs around scattered equipment stating 'DO NOT TOUCH'. Perhaps they were radioactive but the signs didn't say that. After going into some of the areas, he would be ordered to have a shower and check himself for radioactivity. That involved standing on a contraption something like a weighing scale and if the needle didn't go over too far, you were alright. At least that's what he was told.

The generators were used to provide the electric power for the tests. Mostly, as far as he knew, they were testing triggering mechanisms. From time to time there would be relatively small explosions. The tests were part of a series of 'minor trials' as they were officially called. However, not only were they testing triggering mechanisms but also conducting implosion experiments and nuclear accident simulations. Many of the tests used plutonium. Before any test, a tracker was sent out to check if any Aborigines had moved back into the area. They had been moved out officially, but of course it was their traditional lands that were being used, and there was always a chance they might move back in. They didn't know the risks but then most of the non-scientists at Maralinga didn't know the risks either.

After a time, he moved into staff quarters which meant having his own room. He was also made an honorary member of the sergeants' mess. He felt good about that and the fact that from time to time he was given a weekend pass if nothing much was happening that required his services. So he was able to get back to Elizabeth for short breaks. The R.A.A.F. flew regularly between Maralinga, Woomera and Adelaide's Edinburgh air base.

The high point of his nine month period at Maralinga, was being there for a major 'minor trial'. It was postponed several times because of unfavourable winds, but when it did happen, it was an almost unbelievable experience. He was with others viewing the explosion from an elevated position. They were ordered to turn away from the test site to protect their eyes. There was a huge flash followed by an enormous bang. Then they turned to see the ferocious mushroom cloud. Now I know what happened at Hiroshima, he thought. At the time in England when he had heard about Hiroshima, he had been incapable of imagining such an explosion despite his experience of being bombed in Spain and of the London Blitz.

Not long after that he was ordered to return to the W.R.E. He couldn't understand why and was never told why. He did however get wind of the fact that having had weekend passes while working on such a high security project might have been the problem. He had been seen in Elizabeth and questions had been asked. Of course, leave had been granted by the British authorities not WR.E. Perhaps the political climate of the time had a bearing on his withdrawal from Maralinga. The Menzies Liberal government had only a one seat majority and there was great concern that if the public knew the truth about the so-called minor tests, it would spell electoral disaster. Mistakes had been made. Upper level winds had been misjudged. Radioactive fallout had reached as far as Adelaide, but few knew. Richard's working at the test sites and having the odd weekend off in Elizabeth didn't sit well with the political need for total security. A further source of Government anxiety was that there was an International Test Ban Treaty in place at the time, and the tests, if known about by Russia or America, would have been seen to be in breach of the Treaty. Irrespective of the reasons for his withdrawal, he felt again that he had been treated badly and was powerless to do anything about it. After a few weeks back in the workshop he resigned. It was a bad decision. It was a good job. He was to regret it.

20

ELIZABETH

Towards the end of 1961, Richard went into business. He had been friendly with Harry Searle for some time. They shared the same interest in rugby football. Harry knew that at the time Richard left W.R.E. he was in a good financial position. He put the proposal to him that they should form a partnership and buy Edinburgh Motors in Salisbury. It had just come onto the market. He agreed. They held equal shares. The business traded British Motor Corporation products. It was now the era of the family car and business was brisk. The cars were almost selling themselves, perhaps partly because the area was full of British migrants. There was garage work involved as well, and Richard was well qualified to supervise that and he didn't mind getting his hands dirty. But the job mostly involved selling. Seven days a week and a lot of evening work. However, one or two incidents upset him. One particularly. He lent, over a weekend, his personal tool kit which he kept in the garage to a fellow Pom as a favour. He couldn't get it back. Joan said that the bounder had probably sold it. That soured him. It wasn't just the loss. It was the way he had been taken advantage of. He was even abused and threatened when he tried to get it back. Then the garage was broken into and equipment stolen. Once the novelty wore off he came to realise that he wasn't really cut out to be a salesman. Eventually, Richard told Harry that he had lost interest in the business, and fortunately Harry agreed to buy out his share as the business was still doing well. They remained good friends, but the partnership had only lasted eight months.

*   *   *

Richard wasn't without a job for long. The South Australian Highways Department advertised a position for a maintenance supervisor: heavy road building equipment. He was interviewed for the position at the Pooraka depot and it wasn't long after he had got into telling them about the work he did in the Middle East and Sudan, that the interviewer interrupted him and said bluntly, "The job's yours. When can you start?"

The main project at the time was the construction of a by-pass to take through-traffic out of the centre of the small town of Gawler, which was only a few miles north of Elizabeth. At Smithfield, which was on the way to Gawler, there was a stone-crushing plant which provided construction material. Richard would pick up a works vehicle, a ute, at Smithfield each morning. Drivers of the heavy equipment would also be there to be transported by lorry to the Gawler site. A mechanic, whose job was mostly greasing the equipment, assisted him, but he proved unreliable. He was a heavy drinker and often just didn't turn up. Richard managed to get him replaced. Once the Gawler by-pass work was finished, the operation moved further north to Hamley Bridge. After that road work was completed, the gang was to move to Oodla Wirra on the Barrier Highway which was much further north. It was too far for the gang to travel there on a daily basis. A camp would have to be set up. With some reluctance, because he liked the outdoor work, he decided to resign. Another resignation he came to regret.

*　　*　　*

Now fifty six years of age, job prospects were becoming limited. But again he was lucky to pick up work locally. He got a job in the new Holden car manufacturing plant in Elizabeth; not on the assembly line, but in the works garage. He thought it would suit him fine but it didn't. The main task was the maintenance of the factory's fork lift trucks which didn't involve much more than greasing them and changing batteries. If anything serious went wrong with them, they were sent out for repair. Still, it was a job. The best work he got was when some cars came off the assembly line with mechanical defects. Clutches or gear boxes not assembled correctly. Richard was given the task of fixing them.

During the years he was at Holden's, he found escape from the boredom of routine work by throwing himself into the Elizabeth rugby union scene. It was an exciting time as the local club was in its developmental stage. The Elizabeth City Council had provided an oval at Womma Park for rugby, and the club was building new facilities including a clubhouse and changing rooms with showers for two teams, and most essential of all to that particular code, a bar. Lights were also provided for the two pitches so that night training could take place. When funds ran out part way through the development, the club ran dances to raise additional funds. It raised enough to finish the job. The main reason for this involvement was that his son Duncan had started playing rugby. Both Richard and Joan encouraged him, Richard by becoming manager of the under 18 team, and Joan by going on the club committee and becoming secretary and treasurer. Joan also went onto the South Australian Rugby Union Board where she distinguished herself by holding the position of registrar and doing much work on its constitution. Joan had other interests. She became involved with the Elizabeth Anglican Church and its youth group and was elected by the parish to serve on the South Australian Anglican Church Synod. It was at the local church youth group that son Duncan met Gloria Holmes, daughter of a R.A.A.F warrant officer stationed at Edinburgh Air Base. They married in 1962. They lived in Elizabeth for some months, then they moved to Glenelg from where they could more easily supervise the building of their first home at Belair. Daughter Evelyn had married Bob Phillips, a teacher, also in 1962.

Joan decided on a career change not long after they had arrived in Adelaide. She had always been able to find nursing work, but as there was a shortage of teachers as a result of Australia's post-war migration programme, she decided to train to be a teacher. In 1957 she took up her first position at Kilburn Primary School. She continued teaching until she retired at the age of sixty five.

Richard continued working at Holdens until 1976 when he retired, also at the age of sixty five. Two or three years before he retired, he developed a new interest through a friendship with Jimmy Gibson, a Scottish migrant. Jimmy was keen on running, and despite Richard's age, he suggested Richard should take it up. Richard decided to support Jimmy running in the Gawler Marathon by following him by car and giving him drinks at intervals. He was amazed to see the age range of the competitors. Some looked older than himself.

"If they can do it, so can you," Jimmy told him. "You just have to start slowly, running short distances, then walking until you get your breath back. Gradually you build up the distance you can run without stopping." Jimmy prepared a training programme for him and soon Richard was hooked.

21

BRIGHTON

After Evelyn and Duncan moved away from Elizabeth, Joan wanted to do likewise. But Richard wasn't so keen as the Holden factory was on the doorstep. Nevertheless, the prospect of spending out the rest of their lives in Elizabeth did not appeal to Joan one bit. Elizabeth was a good place to bring up a family but, she thought, hardly the best place to spend the years of retirement when the family had moved on. In 1968 Duncan and Gloria bought a house close to the beach at Seacliff. They thought it a great place for their children, Scott and Vicki, to grow up. Visiting them, Richard and Joan thought the area was an ideal place for them to retire. In 1972, they sold up in Elizabeth, left their rugby commitments behind them and moved to Cecelia Street, Brighton.

Richard became a commuter, not leaving Holden's until 1976. His friendship with Jimmy Gibson continued, and although his regular training run was along the beach and esplanade from Brighton to Glenelg and back, he would occasionally go up to Elizabeth to train with Jimmy just to check on how he was going. At the age of sixty four, he entered his first race, the Bay Run from Adelaide to Glenelg. He coped well and did a few more runs of similar distance, such as the 10 mile Adelaide to Marion run. The next challenge was the marathon; the West Lakes Marathon. It consisted of two circuits, and started and finished at the huge shopping centre at West Lakes. It was literally a baptism of fire, or rather of water, as it poured down throughout the entire race. Joan got soaked as well in the process of providing him with support, and when he finished, they got straight into the car as quickly as possible to get home and dry off. He didn't even get his certificate nor a results sheet for his efforts.

However, he had got the running bug, and entered the State Marathon from Gawler to Adelaide in consecutive years, returning times of three hours forty six minutes, and three hours forty minutes. He also competed in several half marathons and in one further full marathon where he again ran in under four hours.

He never really retired from running. He was stopped. He boarded a bus and the driver took off while he was still walking down the aisle to find a seat. The bus had only travelled a few yards when the driver slammed on the brakes. Richard was thrown backwards, hit his head on one of the seats and was knocked unconscious. He recovered enough to finish the journey which was in fact a journey home. X-rays revealed nothing broken, just bruises. Not long after this he was tripped up by dogs while running on Seacliff beach. It put his shoulder out. The dog owner didn't apologise. He was too relieved that his dogs weren't injured! He was seventy years old when this happened. It was time to retire from running and simply become a serious walker.

Joan's commitment to the Anglican Church continued after their move to Brighton. She became an active member of St. Jude's congregation in Brighton, joining the local branch of the Mothers' Union, an international organisation, which encouraged families to bring up their children in the Anglican faith. After her organisational and leadership qualities became recognised, she became secretary of the branch and represented it at diocesan meetings. But that was not enough. Her support for St. Jude's large choir was something of a passion to which she brought other skills. Her training as a teacher had added to her natural air of authority enabling her to easily discipline the junior choristers. They were always spic and span, as was the entire choir after she had provided them with a new set of robes. Her abilities as a cook on many a choir camp added to the conviviality after long rehearsals. All this time she remained a member of the Synod. However, her health eventually started failing and she died in October 1983.

In time Richard adjusted to this loss, becoming very self-sufficient with respect to day to day living. He remained remarkably fit into the new millenium, largely due to a daily regime of morning exercises followed by a cold shower. In summer, the morning swim came before the cold shower. And in the afternoons, always a long walk. His only serious health problem had been dermatological. He did not know whether it was long exposure to the sun in the Middle East, the Sudan and Australia or exposure to radiation at Maralinga. For his last thirty years, the scalpel was a regular and necessary ordeal.

22

SPAIN REMEMBERS

The friendship between the Bryant and Speight families started in a
very Australian way. Gloria and Kate met as new mothers at the
local kindergarten while waiting for their little sons, and as people
often do while waiting, started chatting to each other. Duncan and
Gloria's son Scott, and Des and Kate's son Ivan, were enrolled at the
Seacliff kindergarten. Both families were new to the district, and
soon Gloria and Kate became good friends. Then the friendship
extended to the husbands. The friendship was cemented by dinner
parties and barbeques, and camping, fishing and yachting trips.
Duncan bought a holiday house on the cliff top overlooking the
beach at Port Hughes which was one of his favourite fishing spots.
The Speights were regularly invited over for a long weekend, which
usually involved the men going off for the day to fish for snapper,
whiting or garfish in the bay or further out, and the women relax-
ing, and at low tide, going for long walks and talks. Richard, who
was now living on his own, was usually included in the same week-
ends. The Speights delighted in listening to his stories. Kate, a
Spanish graduate and teacher, particularly enjoyed his recollections
of the Spanish Civil War. Des enjoyed the war stories too, but also
his many sea and desert tales. They were also from the north of

England and felt an affinity with Richard because of this. However, his stories were never in chronological order, and the only context was something that had just happened or just been said which triggered Richard's recollection of some incident in his past.

"When I retire," said Des on many an occasion, "I would like to record all your adventures and see if I can write a book about them."

Duncan thought it was a good idea, but initially Richard was reluctant.

"I'd have to tell everything, wouldn't I?"

Duncan knew there were some events in his father's life that he felt bad about. Nevertheless he was keen for his father's story to be told and he encouraged him to agree to the project. Finally Richard had a change of heart and did agree. So in 1997 Des started tape recording all that he could recollect of his life's experiences. His memory was formidable, but of course there were many gaps.

When it came to writing up the story, Des decided to deal with his Spanish Civil War experiences first. Richard had in his possession documentation which authenticated his activities in the war, particularly his Brigade service book. He also brought along to one of the regular Monday morning sessions a news item which had been cut out of the December 1 1995 edition of The Advertiser, Adelaide's daily newspaper. The brief item from the world news column was titled, 'SPAIN HONORS REPUBLICAN HEROES'. The item read as follows:

> MADRID: Spain is to grant citizenship to all those who fought in the International Brigades for the republic against General Franco's nationalist forces in the 1936-39 civil war. It honors a pledge by the republic's president which could not be honored when Franco won.

239

Des asked if he had done anything about obtaining Spanish nationality. He admitted that he hadn't as he didn't know how to go about doing it. Kate came into the discussion at this point and said that as she had recently met the Honorary Spanish Consul for South Australia, Joaquín Artacho Peralta, at one of the Spanish Teachers' Association committee meetings, she could easily direct inquiries to him if Richard wanted the matter to be pursued on his behalf. He did. An appointment was made with the Honorary Consul. He was most enthusiastic about Richard's experiences as a Brigader, and his request for Spanish nationality. It was agreed that Des would write a formal letter on Richard's behalf, seeking Spanish nationality for him, and include photocopies of documents authenticating his Civil War service. The Honorary Consul forwarded this to the Spanish Consul General in Melbourne, Victoria, who promptly wrote back advising that if Richard wished to proceed with his request, he would have to meet the requirements of the Spanish Civil Code which included swearing allegiance to the King of Spain, the Constitution and the laws of Spain. Richard was now determined and made the journey to Melbourne with Des to sign the papers before the Consul General, Señor Arturo Reig-Tapia, after which they were both generously wined and dined. At Flinders Street Railway Station, Arturo twice embraced Richard, as he bade him a reluctant farewell.

In reply to a letter from Des thanking him for his hospitality, Arturo wrote, "I have read many stories about the International Brigades. I was, and still am, amazed at how so many young people from all over the world came to a country they hardly knew and risked and lost their lives to preserve democracy against the black threat of fascism. I never thought that one day I would have the great pleasure of seeing one of those young men before me, with his heart still full of love for my country."

That letter was sent in May 1998 and Richard waited and waited for something to happen. A whole year elapsed before the South Australian Honorary Consul requested to see him urgently. He was told he was to receive a special honour from Juan Carlos I, King of Spain. Joaquín brought out the best Spanish wine in his cellar in celebration.

At Flinders University, on the third of July 1999, His Excellency, Sr. Emilio Fernandez - Castaño, Spanish Ambassador to Australia invested Richard Daniel Bryant with the *Cruz de Caballero*, Knight of the Order of Civil Merit of Spain.

In August 2000, he received his Spanish citizenship and passport.

*   *   *

Richard sits alone in the dining alcove of his Brighton seaside unit. He has finished his morning exercise routine and had his customary cold shower. Now he enjoys his ritual cup of tea and toast. He reaches across to the dresser, opens the drawer and takes out his new Spanish passport. He rubs his thumb absentmindedly across the royal crest on the cover as if to test its permanence. He opens it and is again disappointed to see that the photograph is not of him as a Brigader with his beret and badge. Instead, it's as if he is looking in a mirror. Not 26, but 86. He smiles to himself at the thought of fronting up at the Spanish border with his Brigader image instead. That wouldn't do. He turns over the blank pages. No imprint for Madrid or Barcelona or Valencia. They should have stamped it with Jarama, Brunete, Teruel. That wouldn't do either. They're not points of entry. He sighs and closes the passport slowly. It shouldn't really be an empty book after all that happened there.

The drawer is still half open. He reaches in and takes out the box that holds his '*Cruz de Caballero*' medal. He takes off the lid and picks it out. His mind casts back to the events and people of more than sixty years ago. To Colmenar, Villa Paz and that blizzard. To Dr Minkoff and Dr Barsky, to Fred Copeman and Walter Tapsell, to the Australian nurses and Joan. Joan. He returns to the present and looks up at the portrait on the dresser then looks down at the medal in his hand. I wonder what Joan would have thought about all this.

POSTSCRIPT

Richard's original surname was Smith and he was known as Richard Smith for much of his life. Joan's mother's maiden name was Bryant. Her mother died while she was still a young girl, just as had Richard's father. After Richard had resigned from W.R.E at Salisbury, at Joan's request the family name was changed from Smith to Bryant. Richard's Spanish passport gives his name as Richard Daniel Bryant Smith. He was well pleased with that.

Richard Bryant died on 10 April 2003. He was 92 years of age.

JUAN CARLOS I, REY DE ESPAÑA

Por cuanto queriendo dar una prueba de Mi aprecio a vos

Sr. *Richard Daniel Bryant*

He tenido, a bien otorgaros por Mi Real Resolución de 31 de julio de 1998 la *Cruz de Caballero* de la Orden del Mérito Civil.

Por tanto, os concedo los honores, distinciones y uso de las insignias que os corresponde a tenor de los Estatutos confiando por las cualidades que os distinguen en que os esmerareis por contribuir al mayor lustre de la Orden. Y de este Título, que refrendará el Ministro de Asuntos Exteriores, ha de tomar razón el Contador.

Dado en Madrid, a 15 de septiembre de 1998

244

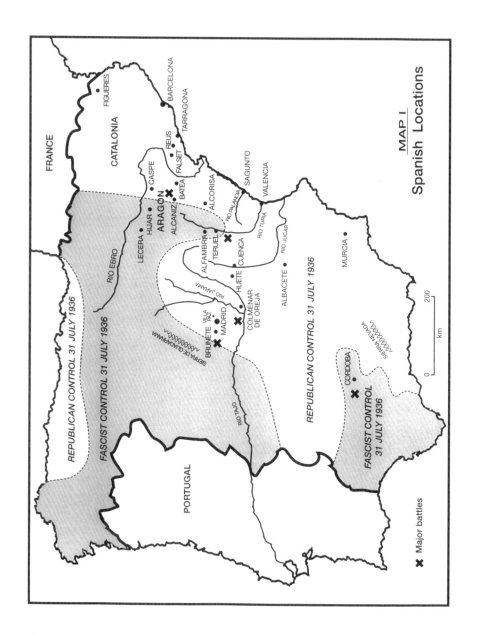

MAP I
Spanish Locations

FRANCE

CATALONIA

FIGUERES

BARCELONA

TARRAGONA

REUS

FALSET

CASPE

BATEA

ALCANIZ

ARAGÓN

LECERA

HIJAR

ALCORISA

SAGUNTO

VALENCIA

RIO PALANCIA

RIO TURIA

RIO EBRO

ALFAMBRA

TERUEL

CUENCA

RIO JUCAR

MURCIA

REPUBLICAN CONTROL 31 JULY 1936

FASCIST CONTROL 31 JULY 1936

RIO JARAMA

HUETE

ALBACETE

COLMENAR
DE OREJA

VILLA
PAZ

MADRID

BRUNETE

SIERRA DE GUADARRAMA

REPUBLICAN CONTROL 31 JULY 1936

RIO TAJO

PORTUGAL

SIERRA NEVADA

CORDOBA

FASCIST CONTROL
31 JULY 1936

0   200
km

✕ Major battles

246

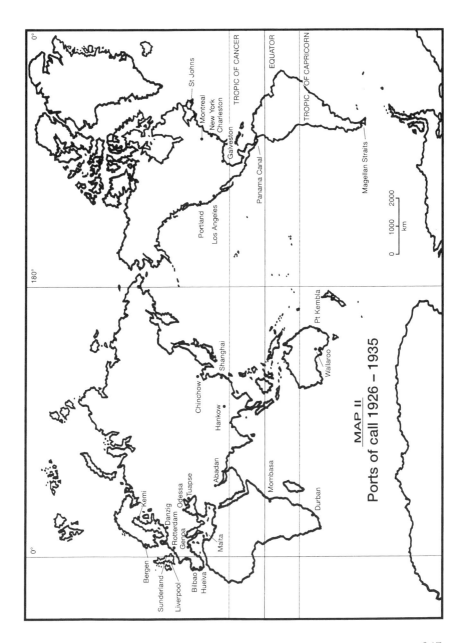

MAP II
Ports of call 1926 – 1935

247

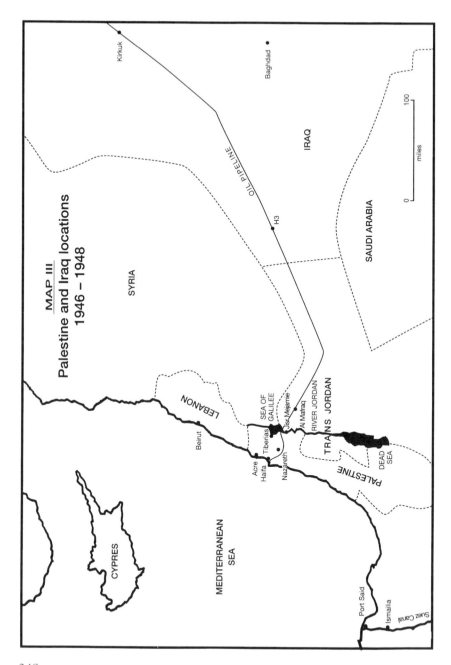

MAP III
Palestine and Iraq locations
1946 – 1948

248

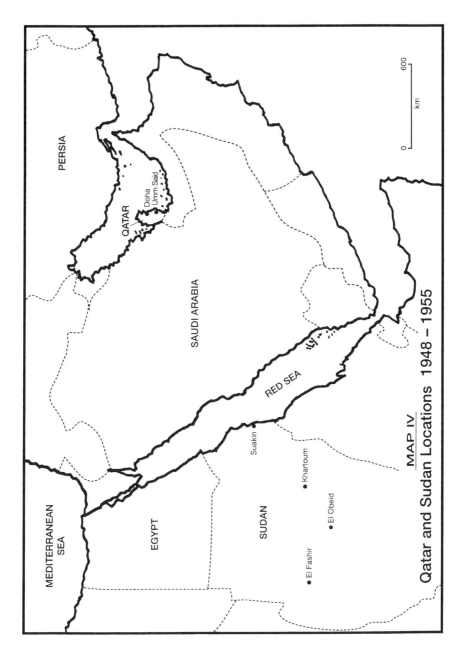

MAP IV
Qatar and Sudan Locations 1948 – 1955

PERSIA

QATAR
Doha
Umm Said

SAUDI ARABIA

RED SEA

MEDITERRANEAN
SEA

EGYPT

SUDAN

Suakin

• Khartoum

• El Obeid

• El Fashir

0 ___ km ___ 600

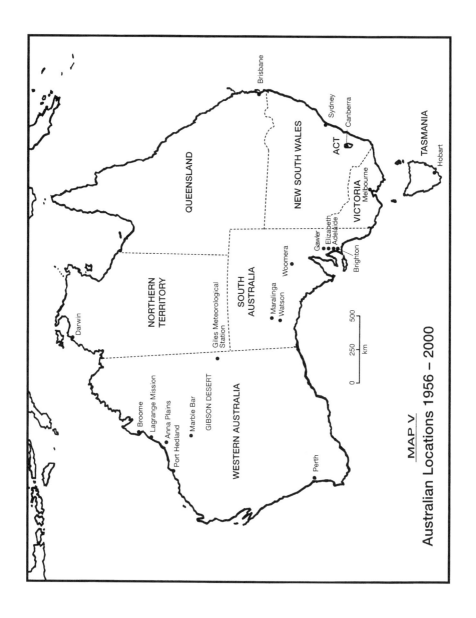

MAP V

Australian Locations 1956 – 2000

250

BIBLIOGRAPHY

The following books have been of great assistance in providing background information.

FOURTEEN MONTHS

Hugh Thomas	The Spanish Civil War, 1961
Paul Preston	The Spanish Civil War, 1987
Paul Preston	The Doves of War, 2002
Vincent Brome	The International Brigades, 1965
Bill Rust	Britons in Spain, 1938
Bill Rust	British Volunteers for Liberty: Spain 1936-9, 1982
Tom Buchanan	Britain and the Spanish Civil War, 1997
Amirah Inglis	Australians in the Spanish Civil War, 1987

SIXTY ONE YEARS

Martin Gilbert	History of the Twentieth Century, 1988
P.M Holt and M.W Daly	The History of Sudan, 1961
Peter Morton	Fire Across the Desert: Woomera and the Anglo-Australian Joint Project 1946-80, 1989
Robert Milliken	No Conceivable Injury: The story of Britain and Australia's atomic cover-up, 1986

ABOUT THE AUTHOR

DES SPEIGHT is now retired from a career in secondary school teaching and curriculum development with the South Australian Education Department. Des has a love of history, although his main qualification is in geography. His wife Kate, who he met at Sheffield University, majored in Spanish. Her ability to speak the language made visiting locations in Spain, which loom large in 'Fourteen Months', invaluable in the book's preparation.